"If, like so many others, you've lost sight of your own life in the drama of tending to someone else's addiction, you may find yourself in this book. Fantastic job taking us into the mind of the addict."

— *Dean Cain, Actor, Producer*

"Wowzers! When I learned that Mike Tourville was writing a new book, I knew it would be good, but this was amazing. An intense read... I truly felt these stories. My heart was pulled out and put it through the wringer. I seriously was broken reading this."

— *Jason Campbell, President, JC Films*

"The stories from Voices from the Fallen sadly depict what is real in the world of addiction. This book opens the eyes to the rollercoaster ride for the addicted, as well as the impact on loved ones that must anguish through the daily battle. Mike Tourville illuminates the importance of this problem, which permeates every level of our society. A must read for those personally affected and for anyone educating themselves on the hidden realities."

— *Paul Connor, West Springfield Chief of Police*

"These hard-hitting experiences are extremely impactful and have the potential to save the lives of those in a similar situation. The extraordinary courage of these individuals and family members to share their personal story with the intent of assisting others goes above and beyond normal expectations. This book is essential reading for those who are at risk or know anyone who may be."

— *William Sapelli, Mayor of Agawam, Massachusetts*

"This book is a must read for anyone looking for insight and understanding into the life of an addict and those affected by it. The struggle is real and the support available is also real. If you are an addict, or love someone who is suffering from addiction reach out. Remember, you are not alone. There is HOPE!"

—*George and Marilyn Ekimovich, Ministry Leaders,*
LifePoint Church, Chicopee, MA

Voices from the Fallen

*True Stories of Addiction,
Grief, Recovery, and Courage*

MICHAEL K. TOURVILLE

Burning Bulb
PUBLISHING

Voices from the Fallen
By **Michael K. Tourville**

Burning Bulb Publishing
P.O. Box 4721
Bridgeport, WV 26330-4721
United States of America
www.BurningBulbPublishing.com

Cover designed by Dorian Cleavenger

First Edition.

Paperback Edition ISBN: 978-1-948278-32-4

For my grandchildren

Lily, Bryn, Nick, and Mikey

ACKNOWLEDGEMENTS

This book would not be possible without the people who bravely volunteered to share their experiences. I cannot adequately express the deep appreciation and immense respect I have for all of them. With some of the names changed, I cannot mention them all individually, but their unselfish disclosure of intensely personal experiences will make a positive impact in people's lives in ways they'll never know.

With love to my wife Chiara, who endured my escapes to the "cave" at all hours of the day and night to write. Much gratitude and love goes to my mom, Paige, for reviewing, editing, and making suggestions, again and again. Thank you for having the patience only a mom can have!

Without my Uncle George and Aunt Marilyn, I wouldn't have known where to start. I can't thank them enough for their encouragement, continuous feedback, and most of all for introductions that led to the genesis of the book. Their energy and passion at Celebrate Recovery cannot be matched anywhere.

A heartfelt thank you goes out to the Jonah family: Kirk, Debbie, Dan, and Karlye for relaying Jack's story, and their mission to help others struggling through addiction through the Jack Jonah Foundation.

I am incredibly grateful to Dennis and Debbie Gonzalez, not just for opening their tumultuous life for all to see and learn from, but for dedicating their lives to help others through their work at Hope for Holyoke and Celebrate Recovery.

Special thanks goes to Lina Racicot for writing her book, *Living with the Little Devil Man*, and allowing me to use Sterling's story as part of this book, and for her passionate work helping families struggling through addiction.

Thank you to Chris Bernier, M.Ed. LMHC LSW CADCII, for offering to write the "clinician's comments" at the end of each chapter, and the informative summary at the end of the book. Chris, your significant contributions are very much appreciated.

To my friends Brianna Dexter, Courtney Caruso, Donna Gorman, and Pam Larivee, who all took time to read early drafts and offer helpful and honest suggestions.

Thank you to the comma cop, my good friend Scott Seabury, for his sharp eye and candid feedback.

And to so many others, too many to mention individually, who offered advice, suggestions, and support for this project. I cannot ever say it enough, but thank you all for your collective efforts in fighting substance abuse disorders.

CONTENTS

PREFACE

Hundreds of books have been written about drug and alcohol addiction, often by the addicts themselves. Many are inspiring, some wildly intense, and I believe all written with a sincere intent to help others through the battle. The more a reader can identify with the story, or find similarities in their own circumstances, the greater the chance it will motivate them to initiate steps toward recovery. If a story is unrelatable, it may not be as effective to motivate change. For example, a rock star's account of recreational drug use may not connect with a person's post injury pain pill use and subsequent drug addiction.

Voices from the Fallen is intended to be different, by including eight true stories that reveal, on a very personal level, a variety of causes and effects of addiction from people of all walks of life. Each also includes perspectives from family members exasperated with their inability to stop the insanity. You'll get to know each of these people, feel their sadness when they fall, joy when they succeed, and find yourself invested in their outcomes. And while stepping into their world, perhaps you'll see something that hits home. If one story resonates, if one message gets through, and if only one person climbs out from the depths of addiction, then this book will have been worth the effort.

Stories describing drug use told in their unfiltered form can be raw, shocking, and offensive to some readers. Depression, death, and broken lives don't often translate into a pleasant read. This presented a challenging task; to convey a realistic, engaging message without turning people off with crudeness and vulgarities.

My goal is for parents and teachers to comfortably recommend the book to high school age children without fear of risking exposure to distasteful content. As the grandfather of four, two of them teenagers, I sought advice from my son and daughter-in-law to ensure that goal was met.

I am merely the messenger of *Voices from the Fallen*. They are not my stories, nor are they exclusive to the eight courageous people and their loved ones, whose message of forewarned danger cannot be shouted loud enough. *Voices* now belongs to the people who powerfully identify with it, who may hear another voice whisper from within that says, "This is us."

INTRODUCTION

When you hear the phrase "heroin addict," it may immediately conjure up an image of a trashy degenerate shooting up in an abandoned alley. It is far from the broader reality around us, but the stigma still exists. No one wants to be associated with that impression, and it may be part of the reason it is not often discussed openly. Stereotypes are changing with increased awareness and education. Those addicts are our sons and daughters, neighbors, friends, and co-workers who live and work and socialize with us every day.

Gender, race, age, or economic stature make no difference. Drug addiction has no boundaries, and there is hardly a family to be found who hasn't been directly affected.

We've seen how it has evolved with alcoholism. A few decades ago, if anyone were to say, "Oh, so and so is an alcoholic."

Someone might gasp, "Oh? I didn't know - I never pictured him that way." *That way?* We have a better understanding now, without the accompanying stigma. And when programs and support groups encourage family participation in the rehab process, people become more comfortable talking about it.

This book provides an insightful look into the lives of a diverse group of people affected by drug and alcohol addiction.

The recovered addicts who volunteered to contribute their experiences found the strength to reach out to friends, family, support groups, or a Higher Power that helped them persevere down the difficult path of recovery. In their own voices, they have laid bare their intimate struggles, spilled out their demons, and expressed deep regrets over their past actions.

It is not only about the addicts themselves. It's how families have healed after being ripped apart, how they overcame financial devastation, dealt with mental illness, or mourned the loss of a loved one. With brutal honesty and courage, the addicts and family members have exposed their deeply personal stories and voiced the distressing truth about how drugs and alcohol destroyed a part of their lives.

Statistics are staggering, and with drug overdose deaths being the leading cause of death for men under 50, it has actually lowered life expectancy for men in the United States. What the numbers don't tell you is the destructive toll it takes on a family or a community. There is no quantitative data that can measure unspeakable grief, or endless suffering through years of addiction. Or the lying, stealing, living with false hope, and repeating relapses... or bracing every day for the call about the fatal overdose. Some parents desperately pray for an end to it all, even to the point of saying, *"Maybe my son/daughter would be better off dead. And we'd all be better off."* Normally that's an inconceivable statement, but when drawn into the depths of drug addiction, there is no "normal," and it can drive you to unthinkable thoughts and actions. These are the immeasurable, and often overlooked effects that go beyond the tally of casualties.

Think differently about their stories as you read, and take a moment to put yourself in their place, or think of a friend or family member going through their struggle. Let it sink in as if it were someone close to you. If you recognize any signs or behavior patterns with someone you know, consider what you would do to intervene now – because tomorrow may be too late. I'm asking you go beyond just thinking, but also talk about it, and ACT upon it. If your gut instinct tells you something is wrong, it probably is. Would you prefer to say something, even if it means temporarily offending someone who is using, or would you rather have a lifelong regret of remaining silent following an avoidable death? A choice to procrastinate or ignore a situation you've observed may be a missed opportunity to save a life.

Recovery is an imperfect process, and the path to healing is long term – forever, actually. Temptations, fear, and insecurity may never be completely conquered, just consciously buried below a locked-in resolve to remain sober. It starts with a decision, but sobriety doesn't come delivered to your door simply because that decision was made. Each person may have their own plan, or "prescription" to overcome an addiction, as there is no standard recipe that applies to everyone. Every path to recovery takes time, courage, faith in support systems, and most of all, a strong desire to persist.

Each of these stories is unique, and despite the common thread of challenges and setbacks, there is hope for a productive and happy life after addiction. Each is told with the intent of helping others pull out of the depths of drug and alcohol addiction, or better yet, prevent it from ever starting in the first place.

A MOM'S 15 YEAR NIGHTMARE

Joe

June 2004 was an eventful month. On the first Saturday, I graduated from high school. The following Saturday, the 12th, I turned eighteen. My mom's birthday was a week later. On the last Saturday of the month, I broke my thumb. This was a pivotal time in my life, the dividing line between childhood and adulthood, and of all those events, the broken thumb had the largest impact on my future.

My sister Lisa was seven years older and had already moved out of the house. My younger brother Tom was still in school, two years behind me. I was looking forward to my "adult" phase, but before getting serious about my future, I was ready to enjoy the summer. On that last weekend of June, my friends and I had a few harmless beers, and I got in a fight with my cousin and punched him in the head over something stupid. The next morning, my hand was swollen and blue. I immediately went to the doctor and was told I broke my thumb. After surgery a few days later, I was sent home with my hand in a cast, and a bottle of Percocet.

This incident began a horrible eight-year ordeal of drug addiction that devastated my parents, ruined my ability to earn a steady living, and almost permanently destroyed my family.

Time after time I thought I had it handled and convinced myself and others I was clean for good. And every time I went back, I would beg them to help me after all the fights, lies, and manipulation. So many times, I'd give them hope, only to crush

13

it as carelessly as twisting your shoe on a cigarette butt. As many times as I quit, I went back. Every single time. Except once.

The first prescription of Percocet did its job of taking pain away. I told the doctor the pain persisted, and he gave me a second bottle. *That was easy*, I thought to myself. Despite my best effort, it didn't work a third time. The doctor refused, saying I should be pain free and off the pills. I needed other sources, so I reached out to a few friends who were doing OxyContin. They hooked me up in no time.

I bought whatever I could get. It wasn't cheap, but I could afford it, at least early on. My tolerance built up and the more I took, the more I needed. I quickly learned more efficient ways of taking the pills from my experienced friends. We'd get our pills, crush and snort them for a quicker high, sit back, hang out, and watch movies. Tuesday night was movie night. Friday night was party night. We'd drink, smoke a little weed, take pills… whatever we had.

The pills cost $30 to $40 each, and I was quickly running out of money. I became desperate and didn't care who I got them from. Consequences didn't register. I was incredibly selfish, but not conscious of it. Deep down I knew it was wrong and had to stop, but I craved the drugs so badly I couldn't function without them. I would rationalize in my brain that I could stop any time. *Never right now*, I'd think, *maybe another day*. It was just too overpowering and became more important than anything. It literally took over my life. I viewed my family as interfering obstacles to work around, to lie to, or better yet, to avoid whenever possible. I became detached, cold, and distant to people who loved me.

Sue (Joe's mother): *Several months after Joe's thumb surgery, I noticed he wasn't as energetic as before. It didn't happen overnight, so I was slow to notice the difference. Then he'd nod off at inappropriate times, like at dinner or during* *a conversation. Those were the first indications. He was working hard at the paper company, but I thought, hey, this kid's 18, he shouldn't be so tired.*

I was also struck by how broke he was. He made good money and lived at home with us, so it made little sense. His personality was changing, and I was getting concerned because he spent so much time alone. I grew suspicious and asked a few probing questions, but he was evasive. I also wanted to treat him as an adult and respect his privacy, so I didn't press the issue too hard.

I hadn't thought about using heroin before, but one of my friends was a full-blown heroin addict, and I was curious. He came over one day and asked if I wanted to try. I didn't really like it the first time but tried it again when I was on my own. That was all it took. The end of wondering. It was one of the best feelings in my life. Next thing I know, I'm off the pills and only shooting heroin. It was so much better, and cheaper too.

Sue: *About a year had gone by and I hadn't noticed any change. Joe was in his bedroom one night and I called him from the kitchen. He didn't answer, so I went to his room and opened the door. What I saw took my breath away. He had a needle and syringe in his hand and was about to shoot heroin in his veins. I screamed at him to put it down. "Just let me finish," he desperately repeated. "Go away and let me finish!" I refused, and he begged me to leave. He was panicking because I was depriving him of the high he was anticipating. I had never seen him like this before. I told him I would not sit there and let him shoot himself up. We argued, and he left. It was not a pretty scene.*

He stayed out all night, and when he returned in the morning, he refused to talk about it. And when he started talking, he lied. He said he was stopping, telling me all the things I wanted to hear. He wanted to appease me just to get me off his back. I knew he was lying, and we continued to find needles around the house – even in plain sight. He was careless and disrespectful, and I didn't know if he was being defiant or stupid. Either way, he didn't seem to care.

Whenever my parents gave me a hard time, I would leave, that's all. I had no defense, no rational argument, so walking away was the easy thing to do. Only when I had nowhere to go, and no options, I'd pretend to give in. Complying was easier, so I'd just lie to shut them all up. I was going to work at the paper company every day on time and had no issues. I wasn't bothering anybody and thought they should leave me alone.

Work was slow, and I got laid off, so I was home more than usual. My parents' patience wore thin, and they grew angrier with me by the day. I'd drive them crazy for a few days, get in a fight, and leave. Even my brother was on my case, and I couldn't take it any longer. I'd stay at a friends' house, but I wore out the welcome mat there too. I finally agreed to go to detox.

Tom (Joe's younger brother): *I always looked up to Joe, but he was acting like an idiot, a completely different person. When he wasn't home things were fine, but when he showed up, everything turned upside down. Everyone seemed mad at each other, with lots of shouting and slamming doors. It was miserable and I couldn't stand him being around.*

Sue: *When Joe agreed to go to detox, we were hopeful. Looking back, we were a little naïve too, as he'd get out, and in a short time start using again. The cycle continued; months of struggling, false promises, hopeful days, only to be followed by painful relapses.*

Some nurses at detox were amazed at how low my blood pressure was and thought I should be dead for the amount I was using. My motivation for going to detox wasn't because I wanted to stop using drugs, I just wanted a place to sleep without being harassed.

I got a few odd jobs and even worked at my dad's shop for a while. I showed up on time, did my job, but was mentally absent. I functioned all day just to get through, while all I thought about was getting enough money to buy more heroin. Any money I earned went straight to the habit.

Mark (Joe's dad): *One morning I was getting out of the shower with my towel and caught Joe in our bedroom going through my pants and wallet looking for money. I yelled at him to get out and he ran like a scared dog. I had to wonder, Who WAS this guy? This child Sue and I brought up was a complete stranger to us.*

Sue: *It was after midnight and something woke me from a sound sleep. It wasn't the sound, but more like a weird sensation that stirred me awake. I opened my eyes slowly without moving a muscle. Through the darkness I saw Joe on his stomach, creeping along in slow motion, like a trained Navy SEAL crawling undetected through a swamp in enemy territory. It seemed surreal until I saw him slowly extend his arms to my dresser, where my pocketbook was. Then it hit me like a lightning bolt, and I jumped out of bed and shouted, "Joe!" He jumped and ran out. We had a terrible fight and he left, as usual.*

I was pissed off at everybody. My parents believed nothing I said, and it was harder to get away with anything - it was like they had an antenna and were ready to jump on me for everything. They didn't believe my lies; I was getting caught taking money and they lost all trust in me. I went to a friend's house for a couple days, was told to leave, and found my way to a homeless shelter for a bed. I hated the shelter. I was tired, hungry, and had no money.

Sue: *After about a week Joe came home begging for help. In all that we had gone through, I never saw him like this. After so many visits to detox, we lost hope, and wondered if it would ever end. Just one agonizing defeat after another, with a constant worry that his next use could be fatal. So many days I'd wake up thinking, is this the day Joe dies from an overdose? The thought never left my mind. Mark and I were beaten, and at the end of our ropes. We were relieved when he agreed to go to the Phoenix House in Springfield for a few months. Phoenix House is a nationally recognized behavioral healthcare provider specializing in treating substance use disorders.*

Mark: *When Joe came home we allowed him to stay as long as he passed a drug test, which meant providing a urine sample. One night I knew he was high, and I asked him to pee in the cup. He seemed a little too confident, and I knew something was up. He came out of the bathroom, placed the cup on the counter and told me to dip the strip in it. I picked up the cup, put it back down and immediately searched the bathroom. Within thirty seconds I found a small plastic container wedged in the toilet tank with a little urine left in it. I brought it out and asked Joe if he thought I was that stupid to test "cold" urine? He finally admitted it was his friend's urine he had hidden in the toilet tank.*

Sue: *Nothing was working, and we didn't know where to turn. We made arrangements with family in Texas for Joe to go to a rehab there, one that did not use methadone. We visited Joe two months into the program, and he said he was dying and had to leave. We told him no, and that he was more* *likely to die if he got out and started using again. We drilled it in his head that completing the program was the only way to save his life. It broke our hearts to refuse, but we stuck to it, despite knowing the pain he was in.*

I lost the energy to fight anymore. I agreed to go to Texas to detox, not knowing what to expect. At first, detoxing in Texas was tough, especially with no methadone program. Over time, it was a little easier, because the separation from my old friends meant I had no sources to get drugs from. But the physical battle was hell. It was like I had a bad flu, with cold sweats and body aches. The insomnia made it much worse, and the constant diarrhea was another thing. When getting high you are constipated, and that's what the stomach pain is all about. In Massachusetts they give you methadone to detox, so you aren't as sick. In Texas all I got was Tylenol and clonidine (for blood pressure).

Tom: *I was glad Joe went away. Finally, some peace around here. I saw what he was doing to our parents, and I was mad at him for stressing them out. They didn't deserve any of that.*

Four months into my stay, I had an unexpected scare. I was out biking with a few girls I had met at detox and we came across a copperhead snake. Thinking it was harmless, I tried to pick it up with a stick. Like a lightning bolt, it sprung up and bit me in my right hand. My hand swelled like a boxing glove and they rushed me to the hospital. I was later told the smaller copperhead snakes are typically more venomous. I spent spend four days in the hospital, three of them in Intensive Care.

Upon release, I was told I would have died if not treated. The bill was over $79,000 for treatment and antidote. The worst part for me was I could not take the pain pills during my stay because of my withdrawal. Only non-narcotic medicine could be used.

I went back to the detox facility to finish my last month and then moved in with my aunt. I stayed clean and stuck around for a few more months. I was in Texas seven months. I came home to get back to work and start fresh.

Sue: *Joe was home less than a month and relapsed. We had an argument; he took off in his car, and we didn't hear from him for three days. I prayed he was safe, and remember wishing he would get arrested, so at least we'd know he was contained and under supervision. I'd rather him in jail than left on his own to use drugs on the streets. I wasn't sure how much more of this I'd be able to take before I collapsed myself. I was fearful of Joe dying and often wondered if it would kill me before it killed him.*

In Texas it was easier, but coming home I couldn't escape the old environment. The places, people, and pressures were right in front of me, and it sucked me back in. But it wasn't the same. I was just sick and getting sicker, so I went to rehab again to get on a methadone program. I didn't know what else to do. When I got out, I didn't drink or smoke weed. I went to meetings for a year and made some new friends.

I went on the methadone program because I believed in my head it was the only way I would stop. Getting off methadone to me was ten time worse. The body pain and diarrhea lasted a good year. I was feeling lousy every day, but my plan was to do it for six months and get off, and I was determined to stick with it. My counselor tried talking me into staying on, but I started weaning myself off. The difference this time, was I was deciding myself – it wasn't my parents, or a counselor, or anyone else – just me. It wasn't easy, but within two months I just didn't go back. After eight years of using, here I am today, eight years clean.

When I was getting high, I was never scared. It just always felt so good, I didn't have a care in the world. While that might sound appealing, it's not real, it's hiding behind a false protective wall. Stress and worry are part of life and are normal to help you cope with day-to-day challenges. Escaping reality only delays facing problems that don't go away just because you hide from them.

Living a clean and healthy life is immensely better, but I have a lingering fear if I ever need treatment that requires pain medication, I will struggle. My current job is physically hard on my body, and one day down the road I might need something to deal with pain. That's the scariest feeling ever – if I'm injured, I cannot take anything. I can live with that if it means being alive and sober.

Sue: *Joe had been clean well over a year when his brother Tom started. Finding evidence of Tom using, I was so devastated I blocked it out. I can picture those little blue pills as clear as day. I remember finding them in his pockets & cigarette packs. Why I was looking I really don't know, maybe when doing laundry. I remember his girlfriend at the time telling me to look at his arms, because she saw track marks. When I found little bags and spoons, I really started losing it. I wasn't sure how I was going to go through this again, and I just wanted to die.*

He would not talk to me about anything. I believe in my heart he hated himself for being in the same situation as his brother. After all that Tom witnessed with Joe's struggle, I could not believe he went down the same path. Tom went through a period of depression and he had a hard time getting past it, which contributed to him using. I just kept begging him to go to detox. When he would finally get in, I'd feel better. Then a week later it would start all over again.

Twice Tom overdosed and was given Narcan to revive him. The first time the police called me and told me he was found lying by the roadside unresponsive. Someone driving by noticed a "body" on the sidewalk and called 911. The police treated him with Narcan, and an ambulance brought him to the hospital. I drove immediately to the ER, only to find him walking out the door on his own. I was shocked they let him go so soon. He was equally shocked to see me arrive, but he easily agreed to come home with me.

The second time he was found unconscious in his car in a grocery store parking lot. An employee putting shopping carts away thought he was dead and called the police. This time I made it to the hospital before they discharged him. I called the detox center, urging them to take him in immediately. After two near death incidents, I wasn't leaving him alone for one second.

I told the counselor at detox I didn't want him to come home, as he needed to go through the program before I would allow him back. Tom told me how much he hated it there, but as painful as it was, I refused his return home. He was my baby, and I wanted him alive.

Tom was in and out of detox 15 times and spent time in 3 different halfway houses. He had to be homeless first before they would take him in, if they had a bed available. Tom used for about 4 years, but I'm happy to say he's been off since 2017, and off methadone since Jan 2019. He is finally becoming himself again and as much as I want to know why he went down that road, I will never have the answer. I choose to let things be, because I am finally getting my real son back. Both of them! After 15 agonizing years, our family is finally whole again.

Clinician's comments

Family members are typically the first people to see a change in behavior from the person suffering from addiction. Usually it starts with something small, but out of character. Initially, families are often under the wrong assumption that when someone enters detox "treatment" they will be all better and the suffering and the lying and the stealing will end.

Unfortunately, it is far from the truth, and consequently the addiction continues without additional treatment. Detox is just a way to separate the body from the drug for a few days, and when it doesn't last long enough, the drugs remain in the person's system and impairs their behavior. Without good step-down protocols or wraparound services in place, most people continue to use right after detox.

Leaving their immediate environment can be good because local triggers and influencers won't tempt them. Unfortunately, if people haven't learned to deal with the root causes of their use, when they return to their home environment, their cravings and triggers are right there waiting for them.

Questions and discussion points

Why do you think the first few times Joe returned from rehab he started using so quickly?

How important or effective was it for him to go to Texas? And why?

Why do you think he started using again when he was back in Massachusetts?

If you were Joe's and Tom's parents would you do anything different?

FOLLOWING IN DAD'S FOOTSTEPS

Dennis

I wanted to be like my dad. As a young impressionable child, I saw he was immensely popular and treated with respect by the people who came by to visit. And they came often. He was the big man of the housing project—the "go to guy" it seemed, for everything. He was stern, with an air of authority you didn't dare defy. As much as I wanted to be loved by him, I felt unloved, unwanted, and less important than anything else he had going on. Despite this, I aspired to be as important as he was and receive the same recognition from friends and neighbors.

Ours was a tough neighborhood in the north end of Springfield, Massachusetts. I had no idea it was any different from other communities because it was all I knew. It was our own little world, and we all found ways to survive. And my father survived by becoming the friendly neighborhood pot dealer. And yes, I became just like my dad. Selling pot became my job, my income, and more importantly, it gave me a sense of being needed. I didn't recognize it then, but the choice of following my dad's footsteps would lead me into the nightmare of drug addiction and losing a huge part of my life.

Growing up, my older brother was the wild and rebellious one, and as a result my mother was over-protective of me. Even though I was bigger than most kids my age, I was quiet and timid. I was made fun of, and bullied, and accepted it all without fighting back.

One event changed everything. We were playing kickball, and I accidently kicked the ball into the head of another kid. He wanted to fight, and I didn't want to. The first thing I thought was my mom would be mad at me. But the other kids started laughing and shouting, "Fight! Fight!" The pressure was too much, and I went at him. Fortunately, I was bigger, and over-powered him and won the fight convincingly. That gave me confidence I never had before. After that incident, I looked for fights, and found them easily. Even at that young age this new sense of power gave me a rush, and I turned into the neighborhood bully. But it was better than *being* bullied. I felt invincible and walked around like a big shit. Underneath this tough front, I still had a lot of insecurities and anxiety.

My confidence grew, and I took more risks. I even stole stuff from grocery stores. It was a game, and I welcomed the challenge. Consequences didn't matter at all. I'd just think of better ways to steal and got to be extremely good at it. It was fun and exciting, and I just didn't care if I got caught. I was restless and did whatever I wanted without fear.

When I was about 14, someone dropped off a large package for my father. I had a feeling it was pot, so I carefully opened it up and stole a bunch for myself, then wrapped it back up so he'd never know. I brought it to school and sold it. I eventually tried it and discovered it helped me escape my fears and anxiety. Then I began taking other things from my father; cigarettes, pot, and a little money here and there.

With this cocky attitude, I knew I'd be good in sports, so I got into playing organized basketball and football. Rather than have my confidence grow, it had the opposite effect, and instead my insecurities grew. Most of the other kids had friends and family supporting them, and they'd all be shouting and cheering during the games. My parents never attended, and no one was there waiting for me at the end of the game. My parents didn't care, and I became angry and resentful.

Even without family support, I continued to play basketball and football in high school. I excelled at football and was one of the first Hispanics to make the All-Western Mass team for Commerce High in 1979. I planned on playing in college and had dreams of going to the NFL.

The environment at home didn't help and I got more involved with pot – selling *and* smoking. I was sneaky, and yet I became comfortable with this routine. Gradually my sports friends disappeared, and my new smoking friends replaced them. I had a fleeting interest in girls, but nothing emotional – just as an object of desire to fulfill a need.

Schoolwork and football were hard work, and I was too restless and impatient to wait for any long-term reward. My dream of playing in college and the NFL faded. Drugs provided instant gratification and took over. My dream died, and I barely made it through high school.

After graduation, I was aimless, hopping from one job to another, with no desire to improve. Dishwasher, security guard, driver - you name it. During these jobs I continued to sell drugs, and each of my new jobs helped me get new clients. I'd quit and find another job to expand my clientele and overcome my boredom.

I never made much money, but it didn't matter, I lived for the moment, not thinking beyond where the day led me. But it got me somewhere – in jail. They arrested me a few times, and I spent a few months in jail here and there. When I got out, do you think I resolved to quit selling and straighten out? No. All it did was motivate me to get better at it. I'd just think of more clever ways to avoid the police until I got caught again and the cycle continued. Back to jail, where I'd work on devising an even better plan…

My parents were fed up and said my life was spinning out of control. They thought separating me from the environment would work, so they arranged for me to go to southern California with some relatives. I was in the San Bernardino area for about 6 months, got homesick and came home. And immediately resumed my activities – like I never left. I had a pretty good gig, and besides, what else was there?

By now I was in my early 20s and had zero ambition – I played basketball, hung out, and sold drugs. It became my occupation. I just wanted to make a few bucks to take care of essential needs, have no responsibilities, and play with my friends. I was an adult but had the maturity of a 14-year-old.

One night a friend asked me to go to a nightclub. I said no at first, then gave in and said ok. Good decision. That night at the bar I met Debbie, who would eventually become my wife. At first, we didn't hit it off, and I don't blame her – I wasn't the greatest catch.

With no place to call my own, I was living with friends here and there, sort of a homeless transient, but always found a place to stay. Despite my aimless lifestyle, something told me I shouldn't let Debbie go. Eventually she agreed to go out with me, we spent more time together, and things advanced quickly. I moved in with her and it wasn't long before we had our daughter Jessica in 1986, when I was 24. I thought about the responsibilities of being a father, so when Debbie was pregnant, I got a part-time job at a gas station, back in the days when you actually pumped gas for customers. We got a small apartment, and I eventually got a job working as a truck driver. But it was never enough, and I still kept selling pot and hanging out.

The following year we got married, which gave me some needed financial support and security. Debbie worked three jobs, while I was still playing basketball and selling drugs. In a weird kind of way, she accepted it.

Did having our first child straighten me out? Not at all. Drugs were too important. More important than attending to my child if you can believe that.

On her way to work, Debbie continued to drop me off at the park to my "job" of selling drugs and playing basketball.

Some deal huh? One day while hanging around shooting hoops a guy said, "You want to try heroin?"

I didn't give it a second thought. "Why not?" I replied without hesitation.

I tried it and fell in love with it. The first time I used, my "friend" shot me up and I had to give him a little extra money to do it for me (some friend). I quickly learned how to use the needle myself.

A short time later I got sick, and thought, *This shit sucks.* I told the guy I was sick from it and he told me to try it again and I would feel better. I said no thanks. A little time went by and someone else came along and asked me to try again. I still felt like crap, so I thought, *What the hell... it can't be any worse.* I felt better instantly and continued to use more and more. Then I sold it and make some extra money too. Before I knew it, I was addicted, and did my best to hide from Debbie. She had no idea and thought I only smoked pot and drank.

Debbie: *I had always "partied" right along with Dennis since the first night we met at a bar, where we were both drunk. We spent many nights drinking with friends, smoked a lot of pot, and used cocaine. I didn't know about the heroin but noticed there was something different about him when we were partying. Things got worse quickly. One of Dennis' sisters told me he was using heroin, and I honestly thought she was lying. I just couldn't believe it. I confronted him and he of course denied it. This was the start of a long road of denial for me.*

Jobs came and went, evictions too, and we kept moving to escape our problems. More drug use, more selling, and more blowing money. Another year went by and we had a second daughter, Kayla, in 1988. Did I change? If you're beginning to see the man I was, you know the answer.

I was arrested again and went back to jail. I got out and had to go to detox and rehab. The obligatory routine. Get clean, then use again, swear off the stuff, then get drawn back in. But I always sold pot throughout. Finally, I went into a recovery program that worked and I stayed clean a couple years.

I was quite resourceful in talking people into hiring me. With my earlier "success" at the rehab program, I even convinced them I could share my experiences to help other addicts. I was pretty good at it, and for a while I was helping people work through their addictions. I even made some friends at the rehab center, but I eventually left that job too, only to go back to my old routine.

During all this insanity Debbie and I had our third child, a son we named Dennis Justin, or DJ as we soon called him. I had a growing family and a growing drug habit to match.

Debbie: *After we had DJ, we moved to Holyoke in an apartment complex where Dennis was the maintenance man. He was using heavily by then, and we were selling pot and cocaine to virtually everyone in the complex. He was also stealing things from apartments, which he had all the keys to. One day the police came knocking on our door to search our apartment. They had already arrested Dennis, and they turned our apartment inside out saying, "We'll find the drugs even if we have to take the kids' pampers off!" I used everything in my power to convince them I knew nothing. I cried some tears, and they finally left. Once they drove away, I went to the freezer, took out the popsicle box full of drugs and got rid of them.*

I was still working but was missing a lot of days. Suddenly I found myself alone in the apartment with three kids under four. The social worker at the welfare office advised me to quit my job because I couldn't afford daycare to keep working. I did what he suggested and soon fell into a deep depression. Dennis was in jail and I moved back to Springfield with the

*kids to live with my sister. In my mind I said we were done,
and there was no way we could go through this ever again. I
knew he'd never change. But those feelings never lasted, and
I'd always give in. When he got out, we got back together, and
for a short while things were good. He'd get a few odd jobs,
we'd make a go of it, but it would never last.*

A local bus company hired me, which turned out to be a
home run. The pay and the freedom were good, and I enjoyed
interacting with passengers. But the best part was the new
opportunity to buy and sell drugs. Prior to being hired, I was
honest with the owner and explained I was in recovery. He was
still willing to take a chance with me.

I took groups of people to New York, Boston, or on ski
trips to Vermont, and things were going great. My drug selling
business thrived. I'd buy drugs in New York, usually during my
"idle time" while waiting for the passengers to return, and then
sell the drugs back in Springfield. I'd get some serious tips,
sometimes up to a thousand dollars for a long trip, and use
those tips to buy more drugs. Who would ever think a bus
driver would do this?

While in New York one night, after dropping off my
passengers, I pulled over and asked a Hispanic guy on the street
corner where I can buy heroin.

"You lookin' for heroin?" he asked with a disbelieving look
on his face. "And you drivin' that big bus there?"

"Yup," I said. "What do you say?" Now you might ask how
I'd know that a random guy on the corner would be able to get
me drugs. It's hard to explain, but I had an antenna for that
sort of thing. It's called experience.

We did our transaction, and I went on my merry way and
got high. This became a routine where the dealers would say,
"Here comes Mr. Bus Driver!"

Sometimes I'd drive people up to the white mountains, high
as hell. I'd turn the AC on high (even on cold days) to stay

awake, and when the passengers complained it was too cold, I'd lie and say the heat didn't work. The chances I took were risky and I could've easily killed someone. Today, I thank God that never happened.

One day I volunteered to take a group to Montreal, only because I was low on heroin and saw it as an opportunity to buy more. I met a guy on the street outside a bar and asked him about buying. I got the same look when he said, "You're a *bus driver* looking for heroin?"

"Yeah, that's right," I said, exasperated at the question. "Where can I get some?"

The guy nodded and said, "Let me take you inside."

He took me in to talk to the guy behind the bar. It took a few minutes, but I sensed something odd. Here I was, this large dark-skinned man with a white uniform walking into a bar in Montreal, where suddenly I realized it was where men meet men for a good time.

The bartender and I transacted our business, and I went back to the bus. The original guy followed me out and asked if I wanted a favor. At first, I didn't understand, so I asked what he meant.

"You know," the guy says, with puppy dog eyes.

"You mean a sexual favor? Is that what you want?"

"Of course!" he replied, "Isn't it what *you* want?"

"Oh no. I'm not into that," I quickly replied, with my hands waving him off. It was just my luck to get solicited by a male prostitute!

Now this trip to Montreal wasn't quite over yet. I had to make it back through customs with heroin stashed in my bag, and it hadn't occurred to me when I bought it. Coming into Montreal was easy. Going back to the US was a problem.

They asked me to pull over at the border, and I was getting paranoid and nervous as hell. With a busload of people, and heroin in my bag, I began to sweat. They made me open the doors underneath where the luggage was stored, and they walked around with a dog sniffing every inch of the bus. I went back in the bus when the dog started barking. *Oh no, this is it,* I thought. I stiffened up and imagined the headlines: BUS DRIVER CAUGHT SMUGGLING HEROIN.

So much went through my mind; Debbie, our kids, my job, everything. The patrol guy came on the bus and asked who owned a bag they held up. Turns out one of the passengers had pot. They pulled him out and detained him. A few minutes later, I warned the passengers to be more careful, and demanded they don't ever even THINK to do something like that on my bus! I lectured them about the dangers of bringing drugs over the border and how they would jeopardize everyone on board. That guy had a lotta nerve, I said. All while my stash of heroin was right above my head in my little compartment.

That little episode made me realize I had to stop taking those kinds of risks. Not to stop doing drugs – no, I had to *leave* the job to enable me to *keep* doing drugs.

Over the next two years I had a few odd jobs driving locally. I had three kids to support and found it difficult to get steady work. My drug habit got in the way, and I'd get fired or quit on a regular basis. Any amount of responsibility was overwhelming and stressful, and my heroin addiction took over. Through it all I kept selling pot – that was my mainstay.

I was using 3 – 4 times a day, and I spent any spare money we had. It was out of control, and I couldn't stop. I finally had to come clean with my wife. It was so hard to admit I was hooked and addicted. It possessed me, and I knew it had to stop, but I realized I could not do it on my own. I had done nothing to change, and Debbie had had enough.

Debbie: *At this point I gave up and moved back to Springfield for the second time. I was not able to change Dennis, and finally I admitted I had no control over anything. Our kids hated us. I just kept working to avoid the grim reality of our life, hiding it from everyone. Dennis and I grew* *further and further apart. I drank a lot to escape from the emotional pain, and sometimes just to sleep.*

We used to refer to our house as Iraq at the time. It was like a war zone – you would come home and all you would hear was shouting and doors slamming. I have always said the loneliest feeling in the world is when you are living in the same house with someone you are not speaking to. We tried to hide it all from our kids, yet each was deeply affected in their own way. Our middle daughter Kayla was spending more time at her boyfriend's house than at home, our son was already starting to smoke pot and was on the verge of dropping out of high school. Jessica was experimenting with drugs and dealing with depression.

I made all kinds of empty threats, and finally after confronting him about stealing from our daughter, I told him I was filing for divorce. He threatened to kill himself and burn the house down. I told him I didn't care, and I left with Kayla and DJ. Jessica, always her father's defender, stayed behind, scared to leave him alone.

After all these years I couldn't hide it any longer, so I called my mother. Sobbing on the phone, I told her of the big mess I had made of my life and she just said two words to me, "Come home."

When Debbie told me she wanted a divorce, I had nothing to say except, "Well, ok, have it your way." I had no defense, and no energy to fight it. A shrugged off acceptance was all I could muster up.

I was alone in our now barren apartment with our dog Bones, and even he was fed up with me. Pouring myself a drink, I locked eyes with Bones as he looked at me in disgust, and I swear I heard him say: *Look at you, you're nothing but a big loser.* And I looked back at him and said out loud, "Well, *you* can go to hell too!"

I sat in the folding metal chair in my kitchen with the lights off and melted into the darkness. Everything around me vanished, and the still silence squeezed me, as if physically compressing my chest. My senses shut down until I felt nothing but the electricity humming through the walls of the house, and even my blood pulsing through my veins. I was shrinking, collapsing into a hole I wished would suck me in. I had nowhere to go, no one to talk to, and nothing to do but sink deeper into misery. One thought consumed me – I was going to die of an overdose or kill myself.

I don't remember how long I stayed or what happened next, but the next day I called Debbie and said I was going to detox. She gave me a nonchalant response and said something like "Ok, cool." Not exactly supportive or enthusiastic, but what did I expect? I didn't deserve her trust after failing so many times. But at least I told her, and thought it must count for *something*. I asked her for a ride, she agreed, and drove me to detox.

I packed all my belongings in my designer luggage – two green trash bags – and went to detox. It was a ten-minute drive but seemed like the longest ride of my life. We didn't say a word to each other. It was the same detox where I had worked a year before.

My former coworkers greeted me, and I was ashamed and embarrassed. Here I was, unable to fix myself after trying to help others only a short time before. Being a failure at that too didn't do my self-esteem much good. I was alone, and broken.

Sitting on my bed at rehab, I cried and begged God for help. I prayed, *God, if you are real, I can't do this myself. Please take this away.* I was helpless and overwhelmed with fear. I went to the counselor next day and told him I could not leave, and if I did, I would die. He was able to get me into the Opportunity House in Springfield, which is part of the Behavioral Health Network, a regional behavioral health services center. I had been there six or seven years before.

This is when I knew God came to me in a strange way. This funny looking dude with a ponytail and missing teeth (who I later considered an angel), came up to me and said, "Hey, my name's Frank, are you interested in going to a meeting?"

"Hey, wait, I just got here."

But he just looked at me and said, "What else do you have to do?"

"I'd like to sit here and stare at these walls, how's that for ya?"

That smart ass reply didn't faze him a bit. He just kept looking at me until I said something else. "Fine, whatever. Okay, I'll go."

We went to a church meeting called Celebrate Recovery where we discussed a 12-step program, bible verses, and recovery. I looked around and saw something odd – not in a bad way, just different. They were all happy – almost like a bunch of Stepford Wives, but genuinely happy, not fake. And I thought, *maybe there's something to this...*

So, I gave it a shot and continued. Everyone seemed grateful that God was able to change their lives. I saw something new here and had a better understanding of how God can make a difference. So here I am in this rehab program that seemed so different from the others, and my wife had no idea. She had started the divorce process, and we had no contact.

I was an emotional wreck, cried all the time, always upset about something. But I kept going. At Celebrate Recovery there were five older woman who nursed me back to physical and emotional health, and back to sanity. In addition to the Celebrate Recovery meetings, I went upstairs to the church services and attended bible study with these ladies. I had been to detox many times and knew the 12 steps, but never got someone to sponsor me. This time I knew I needed someone to help. Someone stepped up, and we bonded. I finally surrendered myself to the program and to God. When my brother died, my new sponsor George helped me through it, and I began to see a true path to full recovery. I told George I wanted to get in touch with Debbie and get our family back together, but he said not to force it, and leave it in God's hands. I was building my faith and trust, so I waited as he suggested.

I was feeling so blessed by all the love and support, I eventually called Debbie and invited her to church. I didn't get much of a response, and I shouldn't have been surprised. I wanted to share this with her, and all I got was the cold shoulder. I thought maybe George was right and I shouldn't have called.

Debbie: *When Dennis called telling me about his new friends, and how he now had this relationship with God, I thought to myself, "Oh sure, now you found Jesus." I just figured it wouldn't last like all our other past attempts. But I noticed something different about him this time. He wasn't pushing to come right back home, he was patient. We kept talking, but I was more concerned about working on myself and our kids. I stopped escaping through work, stopped drinking, and spent more time at home with them. I got a therapist, even went to AA, and gradually opened up with family and friends. I kept finding excuses and turned down Dennis' invitations to church. I was just so afraid to let him in again, I just didn't think I could take the heartbreak one more time if it didn't work, and was still so full of anger towards him.*

So many times, I had gone back to drugs after detox. So much heartache, lies, and failure. *How many broken promises could Debbie endure? Why would I expect her to get on board so easily this time?* I knew it was different, but of course, she did not. I had to prove it, earn back her trust, and most importantly, as George told me, have faith.

I made a commitment to complete the one-year program. During this time Debbie and I began to talk, and she slowly came around. It wasn't easy, and at times I was tempted to leave the program, but we helped each other through the rough times. The difference was God's presence.

Debbie: *I finally gave in and agreed to meet him at church on a Sunday morning. I will never forget it because I didn't just meet Dennis there, I met God. First of all, I found it strange that these unfamiliar smiling faces were acting like they knew me, saying they were so happy to see me there. I remember thinking, these people must be phony, there's no way they are really this happy. And I remember sitting on the bench next to Dennis, being careful not to sit too close because I thought if I even touched him I would break, the floodgates would open, and I would cry all the tears I held inside for so long. And when the music started playing, the lyrics to every song pierced my heart and seemed to apply directly to me. The pastor started delivering a message, and it seemed like he was looking right at me as he preached about "forgiveness" of all things. I distinctly remember him talking about how Jesus forgives all our sins, and yet we have a hard time forgiving one or two people in our own lives. I cried through most of the service, but most importantly I forgave Dennis, forgave myself, and asked Jesus into my heart fully admitting I needed Him in my life. That was the beginning of our new life together.*

Debbie and I both made a commitment to stay apart for one year to work on ourselves, our relationship with God, and be the parents our kids deserved. We never really knew how to get through this disease of addiction together. There was no instruction book for couples on how to do it and it seemed the 12-step programs simply said *"You have to do it for yourself, etc."*

So, we didn't really know what we were doing, and the truth is, we found the instruction book – it was the Bible. Life was changing, new doors were opening, and we had new loving supportive friends. I even started a home improvement business in Chicopee. We finally paid some debts, our kids grew, and had kids of their own.

I had a new lease on life and reflected often about the life I once lived. I was always searching to fill a void I could never satisfy. Nothing worked – not money, sex, or drugs. I was spiritually disconnected. We had some challenges through the years of recovery, but my relationship with my wife and children is wonderful and I couldn't ask for it to be better.

Debbie and I now council people together with Celebrate Recovery and work together during the day at the Hope for Holyoke Recovery Center. We welcome people affected by addiction, in all stages of recovery. Debbie happens to be my boss, and I'm grateful for that too!

In addition to my full-time job at the Hope for Holyoke Recovery Center, I also work part-time at the Holyoke Hospital ER, where I counsel people with their addiction struggles. My hope is to make some impact on their road to recovery. As I help people, they are helping me.

One day in the emergency room, a doctor approached me and asked about my work with drug addicts. She opened up about her personal struggles with her husband's addiction, began to cry, and said she was initiating a divorce. I said I knew exactly what she was talking about, and I told her she may have been talking about me. I explained my past, and in turn she poured out more details. I felt her sadness as she expressed her fear that they might take her young daughter out of their home.

Between sobs, she said, "I just don't know what to do!" Now, here was a highly educated person, a medically trained professional who can prescribe a cure for any illness, and yet she didn't know how to help her own husband. That struck me like a lightning bolt! I realized how so many of us have no idea how to deal with drug addiction and behavioral health, even the "experts."

Out of the blue, she said she believed in God and was a Christian. This allowed me to share what I've learned about how to forgive, understand, and give hope. I asked if she minded if we prayed together. Here we were, in the middle of the chaotic ER, exposed to people all around us, and I held her hand and started praying to give her serenity and peace. When I finished and opened my eyes, I suddenly became aware we had made a spectacle of ourselves and had the attention of the whole ER staff! Then, as the chief ER Doctor approached me, I thought, *Uh oh, I might have gone too far!* I expected a reprimand like, *Don't you dare disrupt my ER with all that prayer stuff!* Instead, he smiled and curiously asked, "Dennis, are you now a pastor too?"

I was relieved he wasn't upset, and I replied with, "Doc, I'll do whatever it takes to save a soul!"

"Good," he said, "If you don't mind, I think there is family over there that needs you, I'll take you to them." He put his hand on my shoulder and added, "Please hang around after, there are others who can use your prayers and support."

I can't tell you what that meant to me. It also gave others in the ER fresh perspective of me and showed this thing called "addiction" is much deeper than finding a cure in a bottle or a pill.

Our three children Jessica, Kayla, and DJ are doing well and have children of their own. Kayla blessed us with our first granddaughter Alexis, now 9 years old now. Jessica had our second little beauty, Jasmine, now 5. And our son DJ and his girlfriend had a son in September 2020. They are all on their own living happy lives. And when they struggle, they can count on us now – a tremendous change from the past.

They know their Dad is still standing by the Grace of God. My grandchildren do not know the man I was – thank God for that!

It is a blessing today what God has done to change me into a different man, and every day I pray to help someone that day. I am merely a lampstand and God is the light. If I had taken a different path, in the deep dark moments of my life, I could have easily been found dead under a bridge. God turned me from a wretched man into a new man.

Shortly before my dad died in 2008, I had talked with my sponsor about going to see him in the hospital. We talked about amends and all that, but in my mind I was really going to tell him he owed me an apology and expected him to feel bad for all the abuse and pain I endured from him. But when I arrived and saw how frail he was, I got close to him and told him I was sorry for not being the son I should have been. And then we prayed together, and then a friend of my pastor came to pray with him in Spanish. We weren't even sure if he really heard us, but later the pastor told me he had accepted Jesus. He died later that day. Now I know I'll see my father again. A few years later we lost my older brother. I was there for him before he died, and spoke at his memorial service.

My mother is 89 years old and still playing BINGO every week and living in the north end of Springfield. I am so glad she no longer has to worry about me anymore.

After a life of selling and using drugs, I came to realize drugs are a symptom of how you feel and think. At the end, I found peace. And instead of drugs, I'm selling something different these days – hope, salvation, and joy. I MUST tell my story so I can give hope and share a better way of life.

Debbie and Dennis Gonzalez

Clinician's comments

Unresolved trauma comes in many forms and can precipitate substance abuse. Lack of food, money or education can push people towards what addiction can promise them. It can lure them in with the promise that it will meet their needs. This seems to be a contributing factor in Dennis' case. Drugs themselves provide a high, and the lifestyle of the drug dealing, living on the edge, can be an adrenaline rush. The attention that can come with the drug using lifestyle can be alluring to people who have not had their needs met.

Drugs eventually take everything. They take away your family and your friends and your ability to make smart choices. People then feel lost, or trapped, and find themselves in situations with no way out. Under severe desperation, they may reach out and try to get treatment or assistance.

Without supportive nurturing networks it is difficult for one person to recover on their own. So many try and fail repeatedly. It's tough to say what rock-bottom looks like because it is different for everyone, but at some point, it clicks, and people find a way that works for them to recover. Despite Dennis' repeated failures, he did not give up. The greatest chance of success comes after the discharge from a treatment program, along with love and support of family and friends that put the recovery into action.

Questions and discussion points
We heard a lot about forgiveness in Dennis' story.

Can forgiving someone too early – before they hit rock bottom – have a negative affect?

Is it right to give up on someone and allow them to find the low point before getting help? Is it too risky to take the chance?

How much did Dennis' childhood insecurities influence his willingness to take drugs?

Would you have been as complicit as Debbie in allowing Dennis to do drugs? Or hiding them for him?

When is the right time to forgive?

Would you have taken Dennis back?

INTRODUCING JACK JONAH

Jack

My name is Jack Jonah. I am a son, a brother, a nephew, and a friend. All these labels are correct, but only answer *what* I am, and only identify my relationship to others. None of them describe *who* I am.

I am an artist, a musician, a passionate lover of animals and nature. I am a nineteen-year-old college student studying biology with career aspirations as a nurse or a vet tech. My stubborn streak surprises people, especially when they are so used to my usual soft and sensitive demeanor. I can be passionately expressive with those close to me, but painfully shy with others. Vibrant colors inspire me, and I am wildly creative; through painting, making music, and even in my cooking! Some might call me a rebel, a nonconformist, or even emotionally explosive! That's *who* Jack is.

Ever since I can remember, I had doubts about who I was, who I was *supposed* to be, and how I fit in. The discovery was slow, tough at times, but after so many painful years of confusion, confliction, and depression, I finally found myself in a happy place.

No one in my family is without faults, but we loved each other and stuck together as a family. My older brother Dan and younger sister Karlye were my friends, besides being siblings. My mom and my dad are excellent parents and always loved and supported me. We live in a large home in a pleasant neighborhood, and I don't lack for anything. Except maybe one thing – to be understood. Sounds so simple, but it had huge implications. For so many years, I lacked the confidence to express myself and to be "me" without the fear of not meeting what was expected of me.

My older brother Dan had a lot of friends growing up, and, like my dad, played football through high school and in college. I heard many stories about my dad playing for Ithaca and winning the national championship in 1979. It became part of our bedtime stories at night, or maybe I just hear him talking about it in my sleep. Whatever, it doesn't really matter, but I couldn't escape hearing about his football days! Dan was following in his footsteps, and my dad was proud of him. But I think my dad recognized early on that sports didn't interest me. Could it be because I fell asleep during his "bedtime stories?"

Karlye spent a lot of time at dance classes. My mom was a dancer - as was the whole female side of her family - and they ran a dance school in town. Karlye inherited her mother's "dancer body," and was naturally good at it. Karlye was clearly her mother's daughter.

So, where does Jack fit in? Middle child, the oddball, disconnected from the four of them. At an early age, I developed a fascination with art and music. My dad used to draw goofy cartoonish faces and leave them around the house in weird places, and my mom isn't much of an artist, except when it came to dancing. So, I don't know where my interest or talent comes from, except perhaps, as a therapeutic outlet, and a driving need to express myself. Art allowed me to break free from the confines of my compartmentalized world.

As different as I was from both my brother and sister, those dissimilarities were magnified in school. I didn't share many interests with most of the boys and felt like an outcast. I was introverted, but once someone got to know me, we'd become fast friends. High school years were tough and often hurtful, and I had my share of being bullied. It's impossible to explain just how alone and hurt you feel when you're the target of bullying, and especially hard to understand when it comes from people who don't even know you, yet make judgements and say unkind things.

So many times I wanted to jump into a hole and escape. But the escape hole was never available, so I'd just endure the cruelty until it was over. I couldn't turn it off like a switch when I got home after school, so I withdrew. My parents noticed and tried to talk with me about it. I was embarrassed and didn't want to disappoint them, so I kept it all to myself.

On one occasion I was in the gym and a group of guys were shouting and throwing things at me. A few friends heard the commotion and stopped it. They intervened a few more times and eventually word got around not to mess with Jack. My friends were loyal, liked me for who I was, and would do anything for me. I never understood why some people behaved the way they did. This might be why I've always had a strong affection for animals. They love you unconditionally without judgement.

I took art classes in school and my teachers were supportive and encouraging. Much of my work at the time was with dark, deep colors, using a lot of charcoal, and included a lot of self-portraits. Perhaps I was hoping people would see something in my portraits; maybe something in my expression, my eyes, that said, *Here's who I am, can you see me?* I felt frustrated, suppressed, and wanted so much to talk openly without the fear of judgement. I just didn't know how. A few friends in high school introduced me to smoking weed, and I really liked it. It calmed me down and allowed me to feel comfortable and focus on my drawing.

Dan (Jack's brother): *Jack and I always got along well, but getting into teenage years we became distant. We had opposite interests – for me it was sports, and for Jack, well, he* *was a typical nonconformist; artist, hippie, a rebel with a "screw the world" attitude.*

I started listening to all kinds of music and really got attached to singers from decades before I was born – the Beatles, Bob Dylan, Bob Marley, Grateful Dead, and Pink Floyd, to name a few. I often thought about what it would have been like to live in the late sixties and early seventies. I'd be a hippie for sure – a poster boy for Woodstock! The music spoke to me and inspired me to learn the guitar, and piano too. I wrote music and lyrics, and the words flowed on a page the same way colors poured onto a canvas.

What tension my mind pulled inward, my heart pushed out in super-expressive fashion. Inhale stress, exhale relief. That's how it went, until anxiety and depression took over and altered the delicate balance. I didn't quite understand why I was getting edgy, but there was a noticeable change in my attitude and personality. No one understood me, and I was getting pounded by the constant drumbeat of unattainable expectations and unrelenting pressure. I couldn't be what everyone wanted. A line from Bob Dylan's Maggie's Farm summed it up well, *"I try my best to be just like I am, but everybody wants you to be just like them."* It's a shame how they just don't understand.

I took it out on people around me. Even though I knew they loved me, I was frustrated at their inability to understand me. I'd say hurtful things to my mom, and it caused some tension in the house. My dad would ask, "What's wrong with you?"

"Nothing is wrong with me, just leave me alone," I'd answer, and promptly find my way to my room. I wanted to squeeze my head and not be questioned about every little thing. I wished they would stop.

Kirk (Jack's dad): *Jack was having these brief outbursts that came out of nowhere, and we didn't know what to do. He*

was unusually quiet and spent time alone in his room. We were worried and needed to turn to professional help.

Apparently, this went on too long and my dad and mom brought me to counseling. After the first session, they prescribed anti-depressant pills. At first it was hard, but the counseling helped, and I expressed my feelings and frustrations. The pills calmed me down, but hindered my art. I felt flat, uncreative, humorless, like a zombie.

We continued with counseling and my relationship with my family improved. We had some breakthroughs, and I felt the constraints break loose, little by little. I no longer sensed I was disappointing my dad, and he accepted my interests, hobbies, and friends, even if they didn't fall into the box he'd set aside. I was making my own box. We had monumental discoveries and revelations, and I felt like a suddenly untethered hot air balloon guided only by the spirited winds of my imagination and ambitions. I felt loved for who I was and all I wanted to be.

I stopped taking the prescribed drugs and eventually weaned off the therapy sessions. I found much more clarity when those damn pills weren't in my system. They made me sluggish and inhibited my creativity. Smoking weed, on the other hand, soothed me, and I never felt compromised.

The balance was back. It thrilled me to graduate from high school and explore new interests and opportunities. I loved hiking in the midst of nature, sometimes with friends and sometimes by myself. I breathed better, my blood flowed, and I felt rejuvenated. Sometimes I'd take my art supplies or my camera with me and capture something I'd see in the woods.

Karlye (Jack's sister): *Jack had a creative eye and took the most beautiful photos. He could do watercolors, charcoal, or even just a sharpie, and whip up some pretty creative stuff. A lot of his inspiration came from hiking through the woods.*

My paintings reflected a changed mood too. Brighter colors and softer images replaced the dark, sharp, angry lines. Self-portraits were a mirror image of a warmer, happier person no longer affected by inner turmoil.

I hung out with a tight group of friends that included Dawn, Courtney, Coreen, and Aubrey, and my sister Karlye. We called ourselves the smile gang, and each of us even got a tattoo of a smiley face above our left ankle.

Kirk: *I had a hard time with the tattoo but got over it. Another larger Jerry Garcia tattoo on his shoulder came, followed by Jack getting his septum pierced. I had to accept he wasn't following my advice, as he was old enough to make his own decisions.*

When my friends got together, we started drinking quite a bit and often smoked some weed. We soon graduated to doing coke, acid, and sometimes ecstasy. We didn't cause any trouble or hurt anyone, we just listened to music, hung out in the woods, and experimented with drugs, with no regard for consequences. We didn't go to big parties much, and sometimes just chilled in the backyard playing music.

Debbie (Jack's mom): *I loved listening to Jack play his guitar by the fire pit outside. He had a little sanctuary off to the side of the pool – a pond with fish, plants, flowers and stones arranged for his own little Garden of Eden. It was a wonderful place to just sit peacefully and let your stress fade away.*

After so many years, the chains that held me back were breaking. I recognized the same insecurities in other young people and understood the pain and loneliness they were going through. One night my friends Bryn and Nick were at my house and we were talking about how cruel it is when people judge you when they know nothing about you. Bryn was especially frustrated and blurted out, "They just give you a label and treat you according to who they think you are."

"Yeah, and like we're supposed to accept it and deal with it, just because they say so," Nick responded.

"What gives anyone else the right to determine who we should be?" I asked.

From that discussion, we decided to write a play called Labels. It's about having the courage to break away from the identity placed on you by others and knowing who you are without having a "labeler" tell you. This became a work of passion, and we finished writing the play in a couple of months. We felt a great sense of accomplishment, but also wanted to inspire people suffering from insecurities to live their own life without being influenced by the pressures from others.

After high school, I enrolled in Holyoke Community College, majored in biology and art, and made the Dean's List. I got a job at the Boston Road Animal Hospital as a Vet Tech and learned how to draw blood, assist with surgeries, manage anesthesia, and administer medications. At first, I was a little nervous using a needle and syringe but quickly became comfortable. One of my favorite aspects of the job was to be with the animals in recovery when they woke from anesthesia. They were scared and helpless, and I could comfort them and calm their nerves. This work had an unexpected effect on me and almost served as unintended therapy.

Dan: *Jack had a profound love for all animals, especially dogs and cats, and loved that work. All his coworkers liked him, and anyone who got to know Jack couldn't help liking him. He always went the extra mile. He never held back his feelings and was brutally honest. It was a tough love kinda thing with him, and he used it constantly. Jack loved to give* *bone crushing bear hugs, sometimes from behind, when you least expected it!*

I was happy working, enthusiastic about my classes, content with my friends and grew more secure with my family relationships. I thought more about my future and slowed down with the drinking and drugs, as they were affecting my moods and ability to function. I never went to work under the influence of drugs or alcohol, and showed up every day on time. I just couldn't continue at the same pace and expect to advance with my studies and work.

I was getting exposed to different people and experiences, and it seemed like a different world. I felt less confined, more free, and honestly, thought less and less about what others thought. Things were going well, and past problems were slowly melting away.

I met a new friend named Ben, and we soon became very close. When Ben came over to meet my family, they all took to him instantly. This made me incredibly happy and in a strange sense, helped me feel whole, as if all the disconnected pieces of my life were finally coming together. I felt comfortable with Ben coming over, not just because my family accepted him, but genuinely liked him.

I was sharing more with them, but not quite everything. What I did with my friends was still private. One of my friends, Dave, was going through a rough time and needed a place to stay. I talked to my parents, and they agreed to have him stay with us for a short while. Dave had some drug abuse history that my parents didn't know about. He moved in and we were all getting along fine. We'd hang out at home or go to Bear Hole Reservoir to hike through the woods and smoke a little weed or drink. Some things were just off limits to talk about, and I didn't want to worry my family by telling them Dave had used heroin. Why worry them unnecessarily?

On Sunday, April 3, 2016, I spent most of the day with my Uncle Kim. I loved being with Kim; he understood me, easily related to me, and always told me I was his favorite. But then again, he told everyone that! Kim was unique and went by the beat of his own drummer. He helped me realize that I can too, without caring about what others think. I could say anything to Kim without being judged, and I always felt better after spending time with him.

Kirk: *On Sunday mornings I typically went to meet my brother Kim. I'd go to Donut Dip, get a few breakfast sandwiches, three different newspapers (at Kim's request) and go to his house. My Brother Mike would often join us. Kim had been diagnosed with cancer a year before, and we all knew his time remaining with us was short. On one particular Sunday, I couldn't make it, but Jack volunteered to bring Kim breakfast and the papers. He even called me from the store to make sure he got the order correct and bought the right newspapers. When he got home later, he asked if he could come along every Sunday. That meant the world to me.*

On the following Tuesday night, I was upstairs with Dave and he went to his room to go to bed early. I went downstairs to hang out with my dad. We watched a little TV, talked about school, work, and other day-to-day things. It was about 10 pm and I told him I was going to bed to get up early for class. I wrapped my arms around him, told him I loved him, and once he caught his breath from the hug, he said, "Goodnight, I love you too." I went upstairs feeling content, secure with my family's love, and all was right with the world.

Kirk: *I got ready for work Wednesday morning, grabbed a coffee, and drove to my office. Shortly after, I got a call from the police saying I needed to come home. I thought maybe the alarm went off or something, but upon arrival I saw several* *police vehicles, and knew something was wrong. They pulled me aside and said Jack was found in his bed, dead from a heroin overdose. I was in disbelief and thought they were mistaken. Just hours before I was in the kitchen preparing for the day, and here I was wondering if he was dead in his room while I went about my morning routine. It just couldn't be real, and I wished so much it wasn't. How could I have not known he was using? Just the night before he seemed fine, gave me a big unexpected bear hug from behind and went to bed in a good mood. Nothing made sense.*

The police made us stay in the kitchen while they took his body out from his room and onto the stretcher. The sounds of people talking around me faded as the wheels of the stretcher pounded on the wooden stairs, hammering louder with each step, and my head felt like it was about to explode. The door sealed shut behind, taking Jack out of our home for the last time. Those sounds will echo in my brain forever.

Dan: I was away at UMass when I got the call to come home. A police officer I knew called me to come home and would not say why. My first thought was that my uncle Kim had died. But when I arrived home, I saw so many police cars and other vehicles there I knew something else was happening. My dad told me what happened, and it was like a war zone in my brain. I lost it and ran to the bathroom to throw up. I was shocked and had no idea Jack would even entertain using heroin. I thought about our conversation just the night before. I was on the phone with Karlye and she passed the phone over to Jack. We joked around, I called him a little bitch, and he was in a great mood. I thought about the years we weren't close and regretted the distance we had through his high school years. But I was also grateful for how much we bonded over the last two years, and I will forever hold those memories dear to my heart.

Kirk: *Jack had so much going for him, and after years of struggling, he had a promising future. He had a secret and hid it well. I had to wonder where I went wrong – I talked with Dan, Jack, and Karlye about drugs and about the personal experience of friends who had sons who had died from an overdose. I thought I was getting through. Jack had a stubborn ego and an air of invincibility.*

Karlye: *I noticed a slight difference in Jack's behavior a few months before the overdose. I think he used a few times, but I'm not sure. This was one of those things he didn't share. He was spending more time alone, but it didn't strike me as alarming. It's so much easier looking back, and impossible to second guess what I would do differently.*

Kirk: *I feel Jack is trying to tell me many things, and I do my best to listen. I know he is sorry, and he needs to know I forgive him. Sometimes I hear him tell me to let my anger go, and he will take it from me. Through all the progress we made through therapy, the deeply personal discussions, the acceptance and love of his family, Jack had learned to let his fears and inhibitions go. Being open and honest was liberating, but there was still one secret he kept, and it was a fatal one. He thought he was invincible, and nothing at all could hold him back. If Jack had talked about his drug use, there's a good chance he'd be with us today. Drugs are deadly, and death is permanent. So is the grief and sorrow our family will live with forever. The only thing I can hope for is that Jack's story may help others find the courage to be open and talk about it, and hiding it from your friends and family can be a deadly mistake.*

The Jonah Family, Cape Cod 2012

Jack and Dan Jonah, hiking at Bear Hole Reservoir

Clinician's comments

For most adolescents, finding your way in life is part of normal psychosocial development. It's common for them to look outside their immediate family as a way to rebel. This sensitive stage can cause confusion, or depression, and result in prescribed medications like anti-depressants to assist with this transition. Medications can come with side effects, which can be felt, or observed, before the benefits are noticeable.

Drugs, on the other hand, provide more immediacy, and clients have reported to me it made them feel better right away. The negative side effects of some drugs, like marijuana, are not felt immediately, so they may be perceived as harmless. This thought process makes it easier to experiment with different drugs to continue chasing that feeling of being high, in charge, powerful, creative, etc.

It is common for a group of new "friends" to come into the circle to provide a fresh experience to the adolescent. When it escalates to more serious drugs like heroin, it becomes impossible to tell what those drugs are mixed with. Many dealers on the street will mix "their product" with anything from crushed B12 supplements to Fentanyl. These additives can provide a lethal cocktail to someone on the first try.

Questions and discussion points

Jack's parents never had to live through the ongoing effects of Jack's drug use. What might have changed if they were aware?

Were there any signs they missed?

If they suspected drug use, would they have a right to look through Jack's room and backpack for evidence?

For information about the Jack Jonah Foundation, please visit: www.jackjonahfoundation.com.

The mission of the Jack Jonah Foundation is simple: *To encourage, foster, teach, engage and provide opportunities, specifically in the areas of drug awareness, and to provide assistance, financial or otherwise, in the promotion of drug awareness and education.*

The Jack Jonah Foundation is a registered 501c3 charity and can accept tax deductible donations.

BREAKING THE CHAINS OF TRAUMA

Jason

The decision was made. The note written. It was time to go. I ran out the door in a hurry, holding the handwritten letter containing a few cryptic goodbyes and lyrics to a song that summed up my wasted life. I placed the letter in my jacket pocket, hoping whoever discovered my body would find it. I drove off in a drunken stupor, regretting the many times before I thought about suicide but failed at that too. Now things were so much worse, without a chance in hell of anything changing.

I had never known life without being in total fear or utter depression. I battled it my whole life, while it ruined my relationships, my social life, and any chance of a productive career. It's no wonder I welcomed drugs and alcohol into my twisted world. I thought it would relieve the sadness, pain, and mental anguish I dealt with every day. And it shouldn't be any surprise that drugs and alcohol made things a hundred times worse. My life was a complete wreckage, and I'd had enough. I had no one to go to, nothing to my name, and no reason to live a day longer.

This feeling of hopelessness was nothing new. As far back as my memory takes me, something always seemed wrong. My mother and father had a volatile marriage, and when they finally got divorced, things got even worse. My father abused my mother in every way possible; physically, psychologically, and sexually. For her own safety, she moved with some relatives in California. My younger brother Ron (who we all called Butch) and I temporarily moved in with my Aunt Mary when I was about 14. My father, who had officially adopted me years before, was in prison.

It was around that age when I first heard the terms bipolar and depression. One of my aunt's friends was visiting, and I was talking with her about the way I feel. She was especially caring and intuitive, and I remember no one had ever listened to me the way she had. I told her why I act the way I do and explained the feelings that drove me crazy, and she simply said, "You are way too young to go through those emotions." She was sincerely trying to help, but once she told me something was wrong, I understood I was flawed, and it only magnified my worthless thoughts. And there were many.

When my mother was visiting, she took me to a psychologist. I was diagnosed as bipolar, and given a prescription of Zoloft to treat my depression. That's when those terms took hold in my mind, causing me to feel strange and defective. I took the medication for three days, then threw the pills away. I never gave them a chance to work and didn't like the way they made me feel anyway. At that young age, I was still afraid of drugs. I never went back to the shrink. With both parents absent, I had no accountability and no disciplinarian to keep me on track.

My grandmother (my mother's mother) was my only solid influence growing up. She took my mother's place both financially and parentally even as she continually struggled with severe diabetes and other health problems. My other grandmother was protective of my father, even to the point of making excuses for his excessive drinking. My entire childhood I was told by her that he wouldn't drink if me and Butch were better behaved and helped around the house more. Somehow, his drinking was *our* fault.

In 1993, my father had caused a terrible car accident and was charged with a DUI. The people in the other car were seriously injured, and on the day of sentencing they were both present in court. Much to our surprise, they asked the court for leniency for my father. I saw the look of genuine care and compassion as they learned my father was a single parent who had adopted me when he didn't have to. He was sentenced to three years in prison.

The night of the accident I had a conversation with my other grandmother, my father's mother, where she kept telling me I needed to be there for him. She went through the litany of reasons he's a drunk, and how it was my job to take care of him. I understood little about it then, but I carried some guilt for not being able to support my dad as my grandmother insisted. It was a lot for a fourteen-year-old kid to take on.

At the beginning of my sophomore year, I dropped out of high school and started smoking marijuana and drinking, but stayed away from the harder drugs. I worked at a chicken wing shop called "Wingers", but after a year the business closed. A friend of mine who worked for a technical school got me involved with a program for play-by-play announcing for sporting events. I really liked it, and he even said I was good at it. It seemed like a promising career.

After my father's release, he moved into an apartment above a garage in Stafford, Connecticut, and I moved back in with him. I was 17 and worked for an environmental company. Dreams of being a sports announcer faded, but with the skills I was learning at my job, other opportunities became available. One of my father's friends asked if I would be interested in joining the union to work as an electrician. I said yes, but he reminded me I needed a high school diploma to be accepted.

With that goal in mind I attended night school in Vernon, CT and got my diploma at age 20. During this time, I met Terri, and we soon made plans to marry. A few months after they selected me to join the union, she had to move to Maine for her job. I was naïve to think we could still find a way for it to work.

The distance prevented me from visiting Terri as frequently as I wanted, and I overextended myself on the car. I couldn't make the payments and they repossessed it. She called off our engagement, I grew more depressed, and stopped going to work. I was prescribed anti-depressant pills and medicated myself to get through the following days and weeks. When I ran out, I'd get them any way I could; lying to my doctor, faking injuries, and even stealing things and selling them to pay for pills on the street. Any energy or motivation I previously had was drained, and I didn't care about anything – even my job. They terminated me on April 5, 2000 – my 21st birthday.

The pain from this point was so severe I spent the next 3 years in a state of misery and suicidal despair. This is where things spiraled deeper into oblivion. I graduated from prescription pills to doing coke lines and crack with my father and his friends, and slowly built a false confidence I could use drugs without consequence. Drugs would only mask the problems, and I had built up a tolerance. I lost all interest in life and hid from the world.

In 2003, I turned 24 and knew I had to get away from the lifestyle I had fallen into, or more accurately, raised in. I moved back to my Aunt Mary's house and eventually found a job. One late summer night I saw an ad for the Marine Corps and inquired. A recruiter contacted me and convinced me to join by saying it was my patriotic duty to God, family, and country, etc. This resonated with me, especially since 9/11 was still so fresh in everyone's minds. I told him of my drug abuse and loyalty issues to my past jobs, and he told me of his own troubled past and how the Marine Corps helped him become a new man. He sold me, but unfortunately, I underestimated the effects of my drug use and the ensuing difficulty of withdrawal.

In October 2003, just before leaving for boot camp at Parris Island, I visited my grandmother in the nursing home. She was happy I had joined the Marines and said she hoped it would "straighten me out." Over the summer I had visited regularly and watched her health decline rapidly.

On my last visit before I left, she couldn't move or speak normally, but she kept whispering "Help me, help me please..." and of course, I couldn't do anything about it. I didn't know it would be the last time I would see her. To this day, the images of her pleading for help still haunt me, and I have tried to kill those thoughts and memories with drugs and alcohol, but to no avail.

I told my father I would call him when I got to Parris Island and instructed him not to let me know anything about Gram until I completed boot camp. When I arrived, I called him, and he immediately told me she had passed. I was devastated, and the withdrawal symptoms went into overdrive.

From day one of boot camp, I was desperate to get away and find whatever drugs I could, and didn't care what lies I needed to tell. A fellow recruit told me the quickest way out was to say you wanted to kill yourself. So, I lied to the Navy Psych, but when he heard the rest of my story, he was unexpectedly compassionate and gave me an option to re-enlist after a year. They eventually gave me a standard discharge. To this day, my greatest regret in life was leaving the USMC.

I came home from boot camp, moved back in with my father, and continued using pills and cocaine. Jobs were hard to find, but the drugs came easy. On a snowy day in March 2004, I was coming down from the high of smoking crack, when my father threw me a tiny bag with some brown powder in it. I stared at the bag for a moment, not knowing what it was. Before I had a chance to ask about it, he quickly handed me a straw and told me not to worry. "As long as you're not shooting it, nothing will happen," he said. "It's much safer than a needle, and you won't get infected," he added, doing his best to assure me. I snorted it right from the bag. This was my first dance with heroin, and I immediately fell in love with it. From that point on, my already useless life became far worse.

Now, you might think it was a little strange that I was doing heroin with my father. Every drug I've used, I was introduced to by my father. He saw it as his way of helping me out. I had issues; he saw the pain I was going through and didn't know how to handle it. He knew no other way of dealing with problems, so he thought he'd help ease mine the only way he knew how.

The house became a drug hub, and we drew in our share of customers and new "friends" to hang out with. But throughout the flurry of activity we were careful – we would rather suffer withdrawal than buy from the wrong person. We always had an element of distrust, along with a sense of danger. We didn't want to go to jail, but not for the reasons you might think. You couldn't use drugs in jail, and we couldn't allow that to happen.

During this period of reckless drug use, I was aimless, bounced between jobs, and had no ambition. Drugs were far more important. We had a buffet of drugs at our disposal at the house, and our preference was to bump a few bags of heroin because it was easier and safer. "Bumping" was simply snorting right from a bag or another unconventional surface, such as the back of your hand. The needle thing kinda freaked me out anyway.

I went on like this for a couple of years, sinking deeper into depression. I couldn't take it anymore, and even my father told me I needed help. With nowhere else to go, I decided to go to detox. Upon release, it was a mere five days before I relapsed. Somehow, I found work again and then did more heroin than ever. My body became dependent, and it was out of control. My boss was willing to give me a chance and encouraged me to go to detox in Hartford.

In late March 2006, I went to my second detox and got clean. After three sleepless nights into my stay, I was inspired to do something I had never done before. I slowly got to my knees, looked through the window beyond the glowing streetlight, and asked God for help. I admitted I was helpless and couldn't do it on my own. Nothing happened, so I went about my detox business.

My mom had moved back in the area, and I stayed with her after detox because going back to my father's house would only make things worse. It was there in my mother's basement at about 1:30 am when I had a revelation.

Insomnia was always a problem following detox, and the mental fatigue, anxiety, and depression never helped. I was tossing restlessly in a bed in my mom's basement and saw a vision. Now, I don't remember sleeping at all that night, so I'm not sure if this was really a dream, as I felt completely awake. I saw a figure approach me dressed in black, but it wasn't a scary image. There was some sort of a veil above the head with light showing around it, like a silhouette with no discernable features. The message I heard was simply to have trust. That stuck with me and it's all I remember, but it was enough.

The next morning, I woke up and wanted a bible. I've never wanted a bible before, so it was a little odd, to say the least. I found a pastor at a local church and told him what happened. He told me I had been saved by Jesus Christ, and to accept him as my savior. The other unusual thing that happened was I was suddenly incapable of swearing. And believe me, I could outdo the worst potty mouth you could imagine.

I started to attend church services, and many things changed after. But some things did not. I stayed clean for three months until I once again found myself drawn to partying in my father's den of drugs, which by then had relocated from the apartment into an RV he purchased. We began running dope back and forth out of his old minivan.

One of his drug customers was a contractor who offered us a wallpapering job at a hotel in Salem, Massachusetts. He advanced us each $800 dollars so we could travel, buy food, get supplies, etc. We arrived wasted, stayed wasted, and with any additional money he paid us, we just bought more dope. The hotel manager noticed we weren't accomplishing anything, and he complained to the contractor, who was useless himself. Remember, he was one of my father's drug customers, so what was to be expected? Tempers flared, threats were made, and of course, they fired us. The money was gone, and we were left with an RV camper and an old minivan with no gas. My father took the van to ask a nearby friend if he would spot him dope or money. After he left, I remember sitting alone on the back stairs of the hotel, staring out at the horizon, thinking I wanted to just die there.

But then something motivated me to call a friend for help and the first person I thought of was John, a friend from the church. To this day I thank God he answered the phone. I explained the situation, told him I was in Salem, and asked for a ride home. This was asking a lot, being two and a half hours away, but he said yes, and immediately came and got me. My father arrived back to the hotel just as John arrived, and he was relieved to hear I was going home.

Just a few days following my return, our pastor told me of the Rescue Mission in Springfield, Massachusetts. On November 6, 2006, I entered the program and am proud to say I have not touched heroine or crack cocaine since. Following my time at the Rescue Mission, I have only seen my father a few times. It makes me sad because I love my father, but I know what would happen if we hung out for too long. Separation from that environment was critical to staying drug free.

When I came to the Mission and worked the program, I saw an alternative lifestyle than what I was accustomed to – a side of life I never knew existed. So many new ways of love and life crossed before my eyes, and I experienced more miracles than ever. I saw so many lives transformed by other people who had emerged from their own trials of addiction. The most amazing part was seeing people who had never used drugs, sharing God's love to help addicts, drunks, and junkies change their lives.

I decided to pursue ministry, and recognized further instruction and discipline were needed. An exceptionally kind board member named Ken Brooks came in one day and handed me a brochure for the Word of Life Bible Institute in Portersville, NY. The Bible Institute is a collegiate-level two-year program focusing on three core areas: study, life, and ministry. I read it and immediately knew it was a sign. The admission process took a few months, but after submitting my paperwork and essays, I was accepted. In November 2007, I graduated from the Men's New Life Rehabilitation Program at the Rescue Mission and stayed to help with their Thanksgiving and Christmas meals.

I arrived at the Bible Institute in New York in January 2008 and was transported into another realm. I couldn't believe a person like myself was attending college. I took it seriously and advanced quickly in my studies and ministry duties.

In September 2008, a new school year had started, and things were going well. I was selected to be a dorm RA, and started a relationship with Andrea. She would become my wife in 2010 while we were both counselors for the Summer Camp Ministry for older teens at the Word of Life Island in 2009. I left school a semester early for financial reasons, and Andrea and I moved to Kansas City, Missouri where her family lived. We attended her church and worked with the Youth Pastor who also graduated from the Moody Bible Institute in Chicago. I had a woman to die for, a new job, and a place of our own. What could ever go wrong?

Andrea had a sister named Christine who was married with three children. Her husband was pulled over and informed he had a warrant issued in Texas for his apparent involvement in drug distribution. Their entire family went back to Texas to take care of the problem. When they arrived, he was promptly arrested and placed in the county jail.

A few weeks later, my wife Andrea and her mom Ann went to visit them. When they returned home, I overheard an argument in the kitchen. I walked in and asked what was going on. While directing his gaze at his wife Ann, my father-in-law shouted, "You spent all that money, and all the wear and tear on the car so you could bring Christine some drugs?"

It astonished me to hear Ann really did that. He looked at me like I was stupid and said, "You don't really know, do you?"

"I don't know *what?*"

He leaned closer, pointing at me saying, "Your *wife* brought the drugs, and bought them with *your* money."

I was shocked and confronted Andrea. She confessed but tried to minimize it by saying it was only $200 worth of marijuana. I asked her if she was using and she admitted she was. I was devastated, but held firm and told her I will no longer serve in ministry if she was using any drugs. She stubbornly told me she would not stop.

I kept my word, and backed out of my ministry duties. Stupid decision, but I was irrational. Each day I lived in that situation drove me more and more back into my old drinking habits. I was mad at her, pretending to be so righteous, and here I was losing my own battle with drinking. My bipolar condition and depression didn't help matters, as I would go into a rage, overreact, and sink into deeper misery. I lost everything I had worked so hard for, and sank into an extreme state of despair. I left Andrea in August 2013, just a few weeks after our third wedding anniversary.

I got my own apartment in Kansas City and worked as a driver moving appliances for a green energy company. The drinking went from bad to worse and my money ran out fast. In the spring of 2014, Andrea suffered a stroke and needed money for medicine and doctor visits. This depleted both our savings accounts, and my salary was insufficient to keep up.

Consequently, I fell behind on rent and other bills. I wondered how everything fell apart so badly and became completely hopeless. I was beaten, humiliated, and cried for hours alone in my apartment. The world darkened and thoughts of suicide consumed me.

Out of desperation, I called my mother, and she insisted I come to stay with her. I arrived home in April 2015 feeling like nothing more than a shadow. First thing I found was a liquor store, and sometime later, a job. Then another, when that one ended. I began stealing my mother's pills and drinking between jobs, and even on the job. *Why the hell not?* I was depressed and angry, and who cared anyway? An uneventful year went by while I aimlessly stumbled along.

One night, me and my "on and off again" girlfriend Valerie went out to a bar, became extremely intoxicated, and foolishly went off in her car. I blacked out after getting into the passenger seat and was startled awake by the impact. She hit a pole, and I staggered out of the passenger side of the vehicle. I walked around and pulled Valerie out.

I must have blacked out again because the next thing I know I was in the back of an ambulance fighting the medics to take the neck brace off. Two state police officers came to the back of the ambulance and asked who was driving. I lied and confessed I was. I blew a .29 breathalyzer, which is more than triple the limit. In court I pled guilty and received my first ever offense of any kind. I lost my license for ninety days and was placed on probation for one year. You might think this event would straighten me out, but instead it led to me drinking suicidal amounts of alcohol and taking any pills I could find. In an instant, I lost my license, my car, my job, and my girlfriend.

After three or four months I got my license back, which was about as deadly as putting a gun in my hand. Depression, drinking, and driving was a deadly recipe, and I welcomed it. I walked out of the apartment with the suicide note in my jacket pocket, because I did not intend to make it through the night. It also included lyrics to the song, "A Tout Le Monde" by Megadeth, that I had carried with me since my last night in Kansas City. Maybe even then, I knew it foreshadowed my bleak future.

So, as you read this, know my friends
I'd love to stay with you all
Please smile when you think of me
My body's gone, that's all

These are the last words I'll ever speak
And they'll set me free

By a miracle of God, I was found alive later that night by a state trooper. I'm sure when they found me and searched for an ID, they must have seen the note and lyrics in my pocket and read them. I had passed out on the roadside drunk, but uninjured, with no recollection of how I got there. They detained me at the station, and when I sobered up, they gave me back my possessions and set me free.

Months later, in June 2017, I entered the Rescue Mission and stopped for good. It hasn't always been easy, but my faith in Jesus will keep me going. It's been over three years since my last drink, and I choose to look forward rather than look behind. I am currently working on getting my license back and paying off debts.

I have been through too much to withhold the incredible guidance I have received from God. To me, Christianity is a personal relationship with Jesus Christ, and it is paramount to help others, as there have been so many good people who have helped me and treated me with respect when I did not deserve it. The world needs compassion, and the bible provides all the tools necessary. There is a story in the bible where Jesus has

His feet oiled by a woman and the moral was "He who is forgiven much will love that much."

I am currently enrolled in the Association of Certified Biblical Counselors (ACBC). ACBC is an evangelical approach to standard counseling which uses the bible as its core doctrine in helping those in need physically, spiritually, and mentally. Once certified, I will be part of the governing bodies network and receive counselee's as they see fit. I plan to serve as many as possible with the same help God gave me.

My life story must be available to warn others, and Christ's hand at all turns must be expressed. The famous quote, "You CAN do whatever you set your mind to" has a slight flaw. It should be, "You WILL do whatever you set your mind to." The possibility to change can only happen with love, and I hope to help others see that. It isn't just words – it's a commitment.

Several months into my residency at the mission, I was going through my old things and came across the paper with the song lyrics I had carried with me for years. I took one look at it and threw it out – I don't need it anymore!! I am free.

Tout Le Monde, by Megadeth

Don't remember where I was
I realized life was a game
The more seriously I took things
The harder the rules became

I had no idea what it'd cost
My life passed before my eyes
I found out how little I accomplished
All my plans denied

So, as you read this, know my friends
I'd love to stay with you all
Please smile when you think of me

My body's gone, that's all

These are the last words I'll ever speak
And they'll set me free

If my heart was still alive
I know it would surely break
And my memories left with you
There's nothing more to say

Moving on is a simple thing
What it leaves behind is hard
You know the sleeping feel no more pain
And the living are scarred

So, as you read this know my friends
I'd love to stay with you all
Please smile, smile when you think about me
My body's gone that's all

These are the last words I'll ever speak
And they'll set me free

À tout le monde
À tous mes amis
Je vous aime
Je dois partir

These are the last words I'll ever speak
And they'll set me free

Clinician's comments

Most prolonged drug use creates a situation with the chemistry and physiology of the brain that resembles someone who is clinically depressed. Jason struggled with depression and early recovery at several points in his life. It appears he suffered from Post-Acute Withdrawal Syndrome or PAWS which is a series of symptoms that are still present long after the last dose of the drug is used. PAWS can last weeks or months after the last use and contributes to ongoing cravings.

Jason was lucky enough to find a path to recovery that worked for him. There are many paths to recovery that may include detox and programs, counseling, and medication, and for others, the spiritual route. It doesn't matter if someone thinks your road is stupid. If it works for you, it's not stupid. We all recover in our own way, and only we can say if we are in recovery.

Questions and discussion points

What affect did Jason's childhood have on his drug use?

How much did his insecurities influence his drug use?

How important is it for Jason to maintain a distant relationship with his father?

How should Jason have handled the situation in Kansas when he felt betrayed by his wife? Why do you think he backed out of the ministry?

Was he looking for an excuse to relieve responsibility and start drinking?

A FATAL SECRET

Jennifer

On my twenty-second birthday in May 2012, I was telling my mom's friend Kathy I was looking for another job. She suggested I apply at the restaurant where she worked. The next day I met her manager, was hired on the spot, and began working the following day. I had no idea how much this decision would alter my life.

Over the next few weeks, I got to know a few regulars, especially one group of guys who came in for a few beers after work. One of the guys noticed I was new and asked my name.

"Jennifer," I said. "Everyone calls me Jen."

"Ok, Jen," he acknowledged. "I'm Fred, and these are my friends Steve and Mike."

"Nice meeting you Fred!" I answered. "And you guys too!" I only remembered Fred's name. He stood out.

I overhead Fred asking his friends for a ride home, but he wasn't having much luck. He said he lived in Agawam, so I offered to give him a ride, if he didn't mind waiting another hour for my shift to end. After a few more beers for Fred, it was time to go.

We were barely in the car a minute when Fred offered to return the favor. "Wanna smoke a little weed?" he asked. "It's the least I can offer."

We spent some time in his driveway smoking some weed and talking. He told me he worked at the hospital down the street and his car was wrecked in an accident. Fortunately, the restaurant was a short walk from the hospital. He came by again a few nights later.

"Where are your friends?" I asked.

"I didn't ask them to come tonight. I just felt like being by myself." He paused, then added, "And maybe a little time with you."

He got my attention, but all that came out was, "Do you need a ride again?"

"If you can, yes," he admitted. Realizing his error, he hastily added, "But that's not why I came. I thought I might keep you company."

I gave him another ride, and he took my phone number. The "weed for a ride" deal was working out well and became a regular thing. Fred eventually got his car back, but by then we were inseparable.

By mid-August I told my mom and dad I was moving in with Fred. My three older brothers were all married, and I was leaving my parents alone for the first time in almost forty years, but it was my time to go on my own.

Fred and I were comfortable just hanging out with each other, chilling out at home smoking, and having a few drinks. Just before Christmas we found out I was pregnant. I stopped drinking and smoking immediately, thinking I could easily wait another 6 or 7 months. Fred and I planned a small, simple wedding for February, before I began to show. Life was changing fast.

In early March we had a snowstorm and Fred hurt his back shoveling. His doctor told him to stay out of work a few weeks and prescribed Percocet for the pain. He spent a lot of time on the couch but was pain free. Other than being sluggish, I saw no noticeable difference in his personality when he took the pills. He managed through it with no issues at all.

In mid-July, a month before my due date, I had toothache and went to the dentist. He said it needed to be pulled, but suggested I wait until after I had the baby. Maria was born in August 2013. In September I got my tooth pulled.

Now I was the one with a Percocet prescription. The pain disappeared like magic. I loved it – the energy and euphoria was like flipping a happy switch on. Fred kept telling me, "Slow down with the percs, Jen!" But I was skinny, half of Fred's weight, so it affected me differently. I looked to him for guidance and tried to take his advice. On the other hand, I needed energy to take care of Maria.

I became fidgety, was awake all night, and needed to sleep more during the day. The doctor stopped the prescription, and gave me something else, but it did nothing for me. Fred said he knew a guy at the hospital who might help us out. Next thing I know, he came home with a bottle of OxyContin pills. We agreed I would slowly decrease dosage and get back to normal over a few weeks. It seemed like a great idea, and I appreciated his trust. But in hindsight it was naïve and unrealistic.

Things got worse quickly. I was sweating at night, felt nauseous, and jittery. I talked about quitting but couldn't. Instead of reducing my daily intake as we had discussed, the opposite happened. I couldn't function without the pills and was getting sick if I didn't take it. I needed more and more to function "normally."

I went back to work hoping it would help, but no luck there. I didn't want Fred to know, so I asked a co-worker at the bar about getting more oxy. She came through with my needs, but it wasn't cheap. Fred worked days, and I worked nights, so I could take the pills without him knowing. During this time Fred and I didn't see each other much, or even got to talk until the weekends, so I hid it well.

When Maria was about a year old, Fred hurt his back again, this time at work. His doctor prescribed OxyContin and told him to rest for two weeks. Both of us were taking, and we ran out quick. He convinced his doctor, who he knew from working at the hospital, to give him a refill. When that ended, he reached out to friends who led us to a guy who owned an auto body shop with a private room in the back. Now it was even more expensive, especially to support both of us. We didn't go out, kept expenses tight, and somehow managed our priorities, as misguided as they were. We grew more tolerant and needed more. It wasn't so much to get high as it was to stop getting sick. We crushed the pills and snorted from a tiny spoon for a quicker effect. The regular visits to the auto body shop went on for almost a year.

Kathy (family friend and co-worker): *I saw a change with Jen. Her normal "bright-eyed" look faded, and she became disconnected, vacant, and looked right through you as if you could vanish and she wouldn't notice. And the weight loss was alarming. She was way skinnier than before she had Maria. I told my husband I thought she looked terrible, and he said she was only tired from the pressures of being a new parent.*

I was sick of people asking me if I was alright. I don't know how many times I had to explain to my relatives, friends, and neighbors I was exhausted because the baby kept me up all night. I exaggerated that point to cover for my zombie-like state. One day Fred and I both went to get pills together, and the guy said he didn't have any left.

"What the hell are we supposed to do now?" Fred demanded. "You could have told us before we came all the way here."

"Wait, wait...," he replied, holding his hands up to calm Fred down. "If you like the oxy, this will work better. And it's cheaper too." he desperately added.

He showed us a brown powder, and I thought it was some kind of morphine. He said it was heroin. The mere mention of heroin made me nervous, and my expression may have given it away.

"No reason to be afraid of this," he said. "It's safe, cheap, and gets the job done quick."

I didn't know a thing about it and looked to Fred for a reaction. He just asked how to use it.

"Depends if you're scared of a needle!" he laughed.

"Let's just try a little," Fred cautiously replied.

He scooped a tiny amount with a small plastic straw with a spoon shaped end and snorted it to show us how. "Just like that – easy!"

I was apprehensive, but desperate for relief. After watching Fred sniff a pea size mound, I did the same. It worked all right. The guy suggested shooting in our arms for a quicker effect.

"Let's give it a shot," Fred answered, this time without hesitation. The guy showed Fred, then Fred did it for me. I was nervous but trusted him. I extended my arm, closed my eyes, and waited. I sank in the chair with instant relief. All my pain, tiredness, and cares went away.

Kathy: *I knew something was wrong. After so many months, the "being tired" excuse was a coverup. I had been a heroin addict 25 years before and I knew the look. Too many of my friends had died from a heroin overdose and I wasn't about to watch one more die. My old boyfriend, once a vibrant, intelligent person who spoke three languages and had his own business, is now permanently brain damaged. He's still incapable of holding a job after all these years. My best friend lost both her brothers in their 20s.*

So, no, I wasn't going to just fade away, close my eyes and hope things changed on their own. I asked Jen's mom about her condition and she was oblivious, or conveniently in denial, I wasn't sure which. She thought nothing was wrong, dismissed the thought of her daughter using drugs, and was offended at the mere suggestion. I went to Jen directly, and she denied using anything. Heroin addicts are bad liars. I know, I lied all the time and thought everyone believed me. I didn't believe Jen. I asked Fred, and he didn't want to talk about it either. I was getting dead ended but could not give up on Jen.

We were done with the pills. After a few months we lost trust in our seller, thinking we were getting ripped off. The color changed, quality was inconsistent, and we were always disappointed in our constant search for a better high. We sought out different sources and were skeptical of them too. Tolerance built up, and we needed more as our bodies and minds deteriorated and grew more dependent. In our sober moments, we felt guilty and irresponsible. Maria was two years old and we were denying her the attention she needed. Bills were paid late, and debt was piling up. Despite all this, we couldn't quit.

We tried to overcome it on our own, but it wasn't working. Whatever Fred and I did, we did it together – we used together, and we were going to quit together. That was our pact. We looked for a detox center as we didn't want to confide in anyone for fear of letting out our secret. My friend Kathy kept asking me if I was using, but I denied it. She was on to me, and I knew I couldn't fool her, of all people. It was our personal issue, and we'd work through it privately. That's what we thought back then. God knows, it was a massive mistake.

Kathy confronted me and insisted I go to detox. I played dumb and said I didn't know what she was talking about. Then she played the tough card, saying she'd tell our family if we continued to deny our problem and refused treatment. We didn't want issues with Maria, so we gave in, and decided to go. After meeting with a counselor, she recommended we go together. We told some friends we were going away to visit family and asked if they could watch Maria. After 10 days we arrived back home, got Maria, and naively thought we'd get on with our lives.

We both underestimated effects of withdrawal. The detox thing, to our surprise, wasn't an instant cure. Fred kept telling me, "We can do this together, Jen, just a day at a time." His "*one day at a time*" line just meant I'd be that much sicker the next day. I wanted it badly, but my problem was I never got heroin by myself – it was always with Fred. Now that he was stuck on being clean, I didn't know how to go out on my own and buy it.

We argued, and he confessed he craved it too. He wanted to be an example of strength and struggled through withdrawal for my sake. *One more time*, we agreed, just to relieve the sickness and the nausea. We bought more and never brought up detox or the "*just one more time*" topic again. We both surrendered, and there was no point in talking about it.

The next 2 years went by in a blurry haze. We used only at home and kept our secret. Fred lost his job at the hospital, due to layoffs he said, but he didn't want to talk about it. He worked odd jobs here and there, while I worked nights at a new restaurant. Money was tight, and we barely made ends meet. Our parents watched Maria when our schedules overlapped. I don't know about Fred, but when I saw either of them, I avoided eye contact. I just focused on Maria, with the foolish thought that if I don't see their eyes, they won't see mine. If so, they would notice something for sure. My mom said I looked good "… since you've put some weight back on," as she so delicately put it. Well, she may not have noticed my eyes, but was definitely observant of other things.

Something *was* in fact different. I hadn't been sick in a while but started throwing up again. I went to the doctor and – surprise – pregnant again. I cried all the way home, thinking about how I was going to tell Fred. I was terrified he'd suggest an abortion and expected an angry confrontation. We could hardly afford Maria, who was now four, and we could barely take care of ourselves. As I drove home, so many thoughts pounded my brain. *How could I be so careless? How will we possibly afford to feed two kids? Will Fred say he's had enough and abandon me?* Having a baby should be joyful news and instead I felt crushed and all I could do was cry.

At first, Fred said nothing. After a few long seconds of collecting his thoughts, he just looked at me and asked, "Are you happy?"

"I want to be happy, but I'm scared."

"What are you afraid of?" he calmly asked.

I tried to tell him, but burst out crying, spilling all my fears about money, our small apartment, the inconsistent income, my insecurities about Fred's commitment to our marriage, and finally the drug habit we couldn't get control of. He held me as I cried, waiting patiently for me to finish blubbering on and on.

"Remember Jen, we do everything together. I love you, and we'll love this child more than all those things that bother you. We'll get through it together."

I was overwhelmed with relief and had a hard time catching my breath after crying so much. "I'm not scared if you're with me," I said. "And I'm happy just knowing that."

I knew what to expect with the pregnancy, except for one difference. Last time I wasn't a heroin user. Stopping an addictive habit was much harder than giving up smoking and drinking. I had another person to think about now.

Kathy: *Jen told me she was pregnant again, and I told her drug use can have a devastating effect on the baby. I insisted she immediately to go to detox and counseling. She easily agreed, and I helped her get admitted ASAP.*

I did some research and learned more about the severe consequences drugs can have on a mother and their unborn child. Heroin addiction can lead to physical and neurological disorders, or stillbirth. The first thing I read was that if I wanted to give birth to a healthy baby, I should have detoxed a year before pregnancy. It was too for that, but I was determined to have a safe, healthy, and sober pregnancy.

Withdrawal was again more difficult than expected. Dealing with depression, fatigue, night sweats, and nausea was not a fun time.

I went to into a residential detox where they accommodated expecting mothers. I stayed 3 weeks. I was able to maintain my sobriety during the pregnancy, which I attributed to the care I received at the detox, along with a totally different mindset of preserving the health of my unborn child. I continued with counseling sessions throughout the pregnancy. Poor Fred had to work and arrange babysitting for Maria while I was away. Through all this, our heroin habit was still our little secret. I was honest about telling my family I was going to detox but said it was just because of the pot and alcohol.

Fred continued to use. He'd come home from a night out with friends and I'd see the faraway look in his eyes and knew what he was up to. I'd remind him of the conversation we had about supporting each other getting through this together, and he'd say, "I know, I know, I've been good most of the time. I have it under control." I wanted to believe him and honestly tried to. His recreational relapses became more frequent and intolerable. I insisted he go to rehab.

That discussion started a painful period where Fred and I couldn't have a conversation without fighting. We reached a breaking point, and he moved out. After a few months I allowed him to come back, under the condition he go to rehab and the methadone clinic. My due date was just under two months away, and I needed him to be present and sober when our child was born.

When Fred came home from rehab, he looked better than he had in a long time, and for the first time in years, I truly felt we were finally in a good place. Nick was born in July 2018, and we were overjoyed with happiness. Maria, now almost five, looked happier too. We hadn't realized the effect our habit had on her until we saw the difference in her behavior and personality.

Three months later, my father died of cancer. I didn't cope well with his death and began drinking. I was tempted to go back to drugs but used every ounce of strength I had to avoid it. Instead, I drank more and more by the day. I didn't realize how sick I was getting until my mom visited and said I was shaking and looked jaundiced. I was destroying my liver. She drove me to the ER, where they treated me with liver pills and suggested I go to Adcare in Worcester. The yellow skin and eyes went away with the pills, but my depression persisted.

I couldn't take it anymore and started taking pills. A few weeks later, back to the needle. I remember little of the months that followed. Christmas came and went in a haze. During the cold dark winter, my depression hit a low point where I had no desire to wake up in the morning and dreaded each day.

I resisted calling my counselor because I was so ashamed. I felt like I let her down, along with everyone else who supported me. They worked so hard, had so much patience, and never gave up on me. Finally, in late January, I swallowed my pride and called. I couldn't stop apologizing, but they said they see it all the time and were incredibly understanding. The good news, they said, was I called, and they were there to help me again no matter what.

I went away for another 10 days, followed by regular counseling sessions, and a methadone treatment plan. With methadone, I thought, *I'll be ok in 10 days...* as if it's an instant cure. Not quite. Methadone, I learned, is damage control, and, although not perfect, it's far better than taking the risks of using street drugs. Methadone is a maintenance program intended to go on for months, or years. It's much safer option as the treatment is supervised, doses are controlled, and it's taken orally vs the needle. You never know what you're getting on the street, especially with fentanyl in the mix.

I went every day and after a few months I decreased my dosage by about 10% each month. I had trouble sleeping and gained a little weight, but slowly weaned off the cravings. After a year, I just stopped. Not sure what came over me, but I no longer had the desire. Counseling helped, along with keeping myself so busy with the kids and work I didn't have time to think about it. This was an important factor in my recovery – forcing busy-ness and avoiding idle time.

Kathy: *I saw improvement in Jen's appearance and personality. Most of all, her energy. Her eyes were focused, and her skin had more color, and she actually looked younger. She was getting back to her old self and even went back to work. But I knew how this worked and remained skeptical. Fred was hurt a lot and spent time at home taking care of Maria and Nick.*

Fred continued with his methadone, but it was so routine we didn't talk about it much. We didn't have to – it was a normal part of the day, with no need to discuss it.

An early December snowstorm hit us unexpectedly. When Fred came back in from shoveling, he immediately complained about his sore back. *Here we go again,* I thought. *He's going to look for his old friends and get heroin.* I waited for him to come up with an excuse to leave and planned on confronting him. I waited, and he didn't say a thing. *Maybe I shouldn't be so overly sensitive after all,* I conceded, as he went into the bathroom.

After five minutes he came out and my fears were warranted. It was that vacant look I'd seen too many times. It only took me a few seconds to find the used syringe hidden on top of the medicine cabinet. I followed him into the bedroom and demanded, "What's this?"

He was too high to even respond, but I shook him anyway. I was so angry I wanted to scream but didn't want to alarm the kids. "C'mon Jen, give me a break," he finally pleaded.

"You lied to me!" I shouted.

"You have no idea how much I need this. And what choice do I have anyway? Nothing else works."

"It's the *worst* choice Fred!"

"Easy for you to say," he said, averting his eyes.

"We can't go back, and you *know* it!" I demanded.

"I'll be fine." He tried to shrug it off. "I'm only taking a little to stop the pain."

I tried to see his point, knowing the doctor wouldn't prescribe any pain meds because of our history. I caved, as usual, and told him I understood.

Two mornings later I was getting Maria ready for the school bus. I shouted to Fred from the kitchen to hurry in the bathroom. Nick was eating breakfast, and I had to take Maria out to the driveway. I knocked and pleaded, "Hurry up, *please!* We have to go!"

He wasn't answering, so I tried to open the door, but it was locked. I panicked and tried pushing the door in. With my heart pounding, I ran to the basement to get the sledgehammer. After a few hard whacks, the door busted open.

I was not prepared for what I saw. The sight of Fred on the floor, lifeless, with his eyes wide open shocked me. I dropped to my knees and touched his face. Seeing the syringe on the floor and the band around his arm, I immediately knew he had overdosed on heroin. My husband and father of my children was dead. I wanted to scream but knew I had to shield Maria and Nick from seeing their father lying there. I closed the door, and with my heart racing, I took them both outside. I couldn't breathe and needed air to compose myself. I started to call 911, but something stopped me. *Wait, wait,* I thought, *I can't have the kids see all that commotion.* I had one other call to make first.

"Mom, there's been a terrible accident," I said, as calmly as possible. "Fred collapsed in the bathroom and I think he's dead. I need you to come get the kids right away."

"What?" she cried. "Did he have a heart attack?"

"I think so, please come over now." I reflexively went along with my mom's heart attack question, avoiding any need to explain the truth. While waiting outside, Maria started asking questions, and I gathered all the strength I had to keep composed.

"Why did you break the door with a hammer Mommy?"

"Dad was feeling sick, so I had to get in to help him. He couldn't open the door."

"Is he ok? Can I see him?" she asked, with a look that almost burst me into tears.

"Not now Maria, Grandma is coming to get you and you can be with her while I try to help your dad. He needs to rest a little, ok?" My heart was beating fast and couldn't bear another minute of pretending to be ok while I wanted to collapse myself. Just then my mom pulled up and took them away.

"I'll call you as soon as I can," I said hurriedly.

As soon as they pulled out, I ran into the house and called 911. I came back outside, then in again, not knowing what to do with myself. I instinctively thought I should remove the syringe and take the band off his arm, but hesitated. Seeing the band still around his bicep struck me as odd. The first thing you do is tug it away within a second of withdrawing the needle, so if he didn't even have time to do that, it must have hit him instantly.

The police would ask questions and soon figure out I was hiding something. I decided to leave everything as it was. I couldn't take one more second inside the house and went back outside. So many thoughts raced through my brain. *I can't tell the truth to the police and another version to my family. How will I continue to say Fred had a heart attack?*

Suddenly a crushing sadness came over me. Here I was thinking about lying again, while my husband was dead in the bathroom. I couldn't be honest with the police and lie to my family. They would know soon enough, so I would have to come clean. I started shaking and wanted my mom to be with me so bad, wanted my brothers, somebody... but I was alone, crying, and waiting.

I closed my eyes, hoping it was all a bad dream. *Just 20 minutes ago,* I thought, *we were all going about our morning routine and now Fred's lying there dead. It was my fault; I shouldn't have given in the other night. Fred seemed to have control of it, like always. How could he not know this would happen?*

When the paramedics came, they expressed condolences, asked several questions, and took him away. The police asked me for a statement. Once they all left, I knew the hard part was ahead. I had to go tell Maria and Nick their dad died. At their age, I couldn't bring myself to tell them the truth, and would have to say he was sick. *The heart attack story makes the most sense for them,* I thought while driving to my mom's house.

I told Maria the news her dad had died of a heart attack. Nick was too young to understand. I couldn't contain my emotions any longer, having held them in for almost an hour. We all cried in the kitchen until I realized I had to make more phone calls to deliver the bad news.

The next few days were a blur of making funeral arrangements and answering questions about Fred's health. When a friend offered to watch Maria and Nick, I decided to tell my family the truth about Fred. There were hard questions to answer, like, *Did you know he was using? How long has he been doing this? Did you use with him?* I confessed I had used, but said I had been clean for a year after completing the methadone treatment.

At the funeral people expressed their shock, with more questions, and difficult answers to share. My brother John asked the hardest question of all, "Why didn't you tell us?"

"Maybe I was afraid to." I answered.

"What were you afraid of?"

"I don't know..."

"You know, maybe we could have helped," he interrupted. "I was thinking about the kids and what might have happened if anyone knew."

He just glared back at me and said, "Yet, here we are, at their dad's funeral."

He quickly apologized but made his point. That point has stuck with me every day since.

What was I so afraid of? Whatever consequence I might have faced, whether it was my family being mad at me, or Fred having to go to rehab, or – my worst fear – if Maria and Nick were taken from us, it would be temporary. I would go through those things a thousand times over rather than have my children grow up without their father. All my fears of separation and damaged relationships could be repairable over time, and we might have had a chance to be whole again.

Fred's death is something we will never fully recover from. I miss him so much and regret not reaching out for help all those years. My family might have helped, but I'll never know, because I chose to lie and cover everything up. And I'll regret it forever. I want no more regrets, especially when I have the ability to change things now.

This is why I am resolved to stay clean from drugs and turn my life around. I will not have my children grow up without their mother by their side. It's only been a year, and we have a long way to go...

Clinician's Comments

Jen's first indication of a problem should have been when she felt she "needed the medication for energy "and ignored the warnings from Fred. This story shows another cautionary tale about how addictive opiated pain medications can be, and how quickly one can develop a tolerance and dependence on the medication. Heroin offers a far more alluring draw to many addicts who are tired of spending so much money on Percocet and OxyContin. The lies Jen told only helped to hide the addiction so it could fester and grow.

It is common for people to enter treatment and get "clean" from the substance that got them there only to realize they switch and substitute another addition. They use the new substance to compensate and fill in the gaps that sobriety can leave. In Jen's case it was drinking. Being sober does not mean being in recovery, and absence is not treatment. When someone wants to remain sober, they need to work on a plan every day.

The best course of treatment tends to be a combination of cognitive behavioral therapy and medication assisted treatment (methadone for example) for opiate addiction. One may not work without the other, and it may require several sessions, or series of treatments before it finally clicks, and the cycle of addiction, recovery, and relapse can be finally broken.

Questions and discussion points:

At what point should Jennifer and Fred have told their family about their addiction?

Should Kathy have shared her concerns with anyone else?

Why do you think Jen kept giving in to Fred?

Do you think she regrets it now?

If you were Jen's friend and suspected drug use, would you confront her? Or tell anyone else?

Is there anyone you know that might be holding on to a similar secret?

FROM SUPER DAD TO FUGITIVE

Bart

An intelligent, ambitious 26-year-old man married a beautiful woman and had two adorable daughters. They moved into a pretty home, and all the happiness and success in the world was in front of them. Friends and family abounded, while vacations, birthday parties, and sleepovers consumed the weekends and holidays. It was a Hallmark movie existence anyone would envy. Without warning, a malicious intruder came along and not only pierced the picture but shredded the canvas into a million pieces.

A man in his mid-thirties married for a second time and bore a son shortly after. Professional achievement came with hard work, and it showed in the spacious, well-manicured home and new cars in the upscale cul-de-sac. The energetic young man worked long hours but found time to coach his son's baseball team in the spring and summer, and his basketball team in the winter. The family never sat still, and thrived in the whirlwind of work, sports, and school activities. When no one seemed to notice, a venomous snake entered and poisoned the promise of this happy family.

Living in the woods in a tattered tent, scrounging for food and water to survive, a middle-aged man was being hunted by police. He was eventually caught and sent to jail. A mere few weeks later, he was arrested again - while in jail – for breaking a strict rule in the attempt to celebrate his 50th birthday in his cell. He might not have been there in the first place, or found himself in double trouble, if he wasn't drawn to the one thing he could not do without.

A 54-year-old two-time ex-convict conspired to commit a murder with his gang member girlfriend, who was an admitted killer. And despite knowing this fact, he casually shrugged it off, and planned to marry her and raise a child together anyway. They both shared another dangerous habit too, one that consumed virtually every waking hour. What could possibly go wrong?

My name is Bart, and I was each of the people mentioned above. Reflecting on the turbulent life I've lived, one thing is clear: all the good things I had – my marriages, the promises, hopes, and dreams – all *ended* because of my alcohol addiction. All the legal trouble, damaged relationships, and pain I've caused *began* with my alcohol abuse.

For the rest of my life, I will live with unanswered questions that plague me every day. *If I could only go back and start over. What could I have done differently?* And a thousand more *"What ifs"* to stack on.

I could choose to dwell on the past, remain there, and allow it to take me into an unhealthy existence, a bleak future, and most likely, an early, lonely death. I am attached to my past, but I won't let it define who I am now. Instead, I have resolved, thanks to God, family, friends, and support groups, to begin a new life, and do all I can to help others overcome their struggles with alcohol. And for that reason, my story is being told, not for entertainment, but to show the ruinous effect alcohol abuse can have on an individual, their families, and friends. I left a wake of destruction behind me, fracturing not one, but two families, and causing permanent damage to people I loved.

My early childhood was a normal one, until my mom and dad divorced when I was 15 years old. I had witnessed abusive behavior from my dad, remained with my mom after the divorce, and grew into adulthood determined *not* to be like my father. How well I learned from his example was about to be revealed.

In my adolescence, I was not a religious person. I thought little about it frankly, as I had no reason to believe or disbelieve in God. I didn't care either way. I was my own commander, made my own decisions, set my own destiny.

When I was twenty, a single event changed the way I felt about God and altered my attitude about life and death. My 16-month-old niece Lily (my sister's daughter) died of Sudden Infant Death Syndrome. I could not understand how any God would allow that to happen and put a family through such devastation. The funeral was Christmas Eve day, and my brother and I were asked to be pallbearers. While carrying the tiny casket from the church to the hearse, my brother slipped, and one end of the casket dropped. We felt the body slide down and heard the "thud" of her head hitting the end of the casket. I felt sick to my stomach and cursed God and everything he represented. From that moment, I became a staunch atheist.

Six years passed, and it was time to settle down. In 1991 I married Patti, and we started off happy. Our first daughter Theresa was born in 1992, and Emma in 1995. We bought a house, and I worked long hours in the restaurant business. Occasionally after a shift I'd go to a bar to have a few beers and then go home. Patti didn't drink at all, so there was no drinking in the house. So, in the beginning, I behaved and never drank at home. Well, except when she was out. And on those nights and weekends when work pulled me away, I took full advantage. I always thought I was so clever and convinced myself I was fooling everyone. The drinking increased, and our marital problems escalated.

On one occasion, I told Patti I had to work through the night to prepare for a catering event the next day. That was the truth, but while preparing food in the restaurant by myself, I drank an entire 18-pack of beer. Somehow, I made it home just before dawn and passed out on the living room floor. The smell of alcohol and urine-soaked pants permeated the entire house. My wife called an ambulance, and when they came to take me to a hospital, she simply said, "He's your problem now." After five short years, that was the abrupt end of my marriage.

It took some time to adjust to being single. I learned to balance my social life, work, and my ever-increasing daily beer quota. At a golf outing I met Katie, a co-worker, at the bar. We got along well, and it didn't take long for us to move in together. We married in early 2000 and in May 2001 our son Matthew was born. After a few years of living in Springfield, Massachusetts we moved to South Windsor, Connecticut to be closer to our jobs. We made new friends, hosted endless cocktail parties, and I gradually switched from beer to vodka. Less calories, less filling, and vodka got the job done quicker.

We were drinking every single day after work, but never during work. The pre-dinner cocktail became routine, and I looked forward to it. Despite this little habit, we were good at our jobs, and both of us even received outstanding employee awards. I felt fully capable of managing every aspect of my life.

As Matthew grew up, I volunteered to coach his baseball and basketball teams, and got involved with other school activities. These long eventful days were fulfilling and enjoyable, but eventually the demands and pressure got to me.

To escape the stress of working crazy hours, I quit the restaurant field and started a home repair business. My salary was cut by half, but the reduced hours enabled me to be a better father and husband. That was the idea anyway. We cut back on expenses and made it work. Over seven years, I only missed two of Matthew's games.

I never thought my drinking affected my parental responsibilities, so our vodka money was not spared. We made sure of it. I never drank during work as it was too risky. I got the shakes during the day but didn't think much of it. It was most noticeable on the way home when I'd stop at the liquor store. While fishing through my wallet to get the cash, my hands trembled, and I noticed the cashier looking at me funny. The next time, in an attempt to hide it, I'd count the money in the car so I could quickly drop it on the counter, minimizing the exposure of my condition. "Keep the change," I'd say, and leave in a hurry. The shaking stopped after I had a drink at home, yet still, I did not attribute the shakes to drinking. I thought it was the effect of the high blood pressure pills. My body was changing, and I didn't see it. Or I simply ignored it.

The pre-dinner vodka cocktails became a daily obsession, and we always had a bottle in the freezer. After a few drinks, arguments were easily triggered, where irrational reactions led to violent outbursts. We'd eventually calm down, and pretend it never happened, as if our mutual denial made it go away. We didn't notice the irreparable damage eroding our marriage. When you keep sweeping things under the rug, eventually you'll trip over the lump.

One night we were on the way to an event in Hartford and I asked Katie to drive. I was sleepy and wanted to close my eyes and rest while she drove. A few minutes into the ride, I started convulsing and had a seizure. Katie pulled over and when I opened my eyes, I couldn't see anything. I shouted, "I can't see, I'm blind!"

She drove straight to the hospital, and they took me into the ER. My sight gradually came back, and they asked me several questions. One of them was if I drank alcohol. I said yes.

"What do you drink?" The nurse asked.

"Vodka," I replied.

"How *much* do you drink?"

Her skeptical look told me she did not expect an honest answer. I looked straight into her eyes and gave her a direct response: "About a liter a day."

That was enough for them to keep me there for a few days. My problem was obvious to them, although they chose not to tell me right away that I was going through severe alcohol withdrawal. Unless they did, and I tuned them out. I don't remember. From there I went to the detox center for 10 days where I learned all about alcohol issues, 12-step programs, and attended required meetings. That's how I viewed the programs – obligatory, mandatory. Only to satisfy others. I didn't need them. Those programs were for losers, and I felt above all of it.

A short week later, I started drinking again. No, I was not a particularly outstanding student. I was stubborn and arrogant, and felt invincible – I did whatever I wanted, whenever I wanted. The arguments with Katie resumed, and one afternoon, out of nowhere, she demanded I stop drinking.

"No!" I abruptly replied, "Why should I?"

"Because *you* are an alcoholic, *that*'s why. And I've had enough!"

I insisted she was wrong and said I could stop any time I wanted. I just didn't want to. Several months later, I gave up the fight and agreed to go to an Intensive Outpatient Program (IOP) for alcohol abuse. Following the program, I was sober five months.

I cannot recall the event that caused me to drink again, but it didn't take much. Maybe it was an errant remark from Katie, or simply a look I didn't like, or a TV commercial, or a bar I drove by... whatever it was, my weakness was easily triggered. I lied to Katie and pretended to go to IOP and drove around for an hour and a half, drinking instead. I strategically hid bottles around the house so I could sneak a drink anytime at home.

Looking back, I was oblivious to changes occurring around me. One of Matthew's friends asked me why my hands were shaking so much. I said it was my high blood pressure medicine. And I believed it too. The friends came over less often, then not at all. Matthew may have been embarrassed but said nothing. Katie backed off and went along to keep the peace. She even went back to drinking herself and we resumed our afternoon cocktail routine.

One day I texted Katie asking her to pick up vodka on the way home. My phone beeped back instantly, and I thought, *Oh good, it'll save me a trip.* I looked at the phone and saw the word NO in caps. That was it, no other words, just NO. I didn't understand and was pissed off. This was our routine, and she had the nerve to break it. Her terse answer was like a switch, and all hell broke loose afterwards.

I picked up the vodka and hastily poured myself a glass when I got home. Within minutes a heated argument erupted, and I slammed the rolling pin into the fridge. Katie promptly called the police. When they arrived, they asked if I was drinking. "Yes," I said. "So what?"

They took me out into the cruiser. I didn't resist, and they had me sit in the front seat without being handcuffed. At the station they made me strip down for a routine search. Then they brought me to a hotel room, instead of a cell, and I was left unsupervised. It was what they called Protective Order. As long as I didn't have any firearms, weapons, or alcohol.

I returned home the next day, and to say the tension was high would be a gross understatement. For a while I had suspected Katie of having an affair and accused her in the middle of a shouting match. I became enraged and lost my temper, again. We fought, she called the police, and shortly thereafter she filed a restraining order against me. I moved back in with my mom and, of course, started drinking again.

Janet (Bart's mom): *When Bart is sober, he is a thoughtful, intelligent, caring person. Drinking changes all that. When he moved in, he seemed like a different person and refused to talk to me about what was happening. He wouldn't stop calling Matthew, but I wasn't surprised, as his strong stubborn streak runs in the family. I'd overhear shouting between him and Katie and knew he was going to get himself in trouble. There was nothing I could say to calm him down or change his behavior. He seemed angry at the world.*

I called a few times to talk with Matthew and Katie threatened me, fueling my anger even more. She'd had enough and called the police, saying I violated the restraining order. That move put me in the Hartford jail, surrounded by hard criminals, whom I had no business being around. I was terrified, and to make things worse, they served divorce papers to me in my cell. I was stunned, absolutely blown away. Somehow, in my delusional mind, I thought we would always get back to a normal life. I did my time with good behavior and they released me after two months on an accelerated rehabilitation program.

After returning to my mom's house, it didn't take long to go back to my habits. I fought with her and her husband Dan, who is the nicest guy in the world and the last person I'd have a reason to be mad at. Yet one night in early July I got drunk and lost my composure. I made some threats, and we came close to a physical altercation.

I had to leave the house but had nowhere to go. I stormed into the garage to be by myself for a moment and figure out where to go. On the floor of the garage was a tent I had taken out earlier in the day to repair. That's when the brilliant idea hit me. I ran back into the house to grab some essentials from my room; a t-shirt, towel, sweatpants, my pills, and finally, a large bottle of vodka.

My mom followed me into my room, saw me packing things and asked, "Where are you going now?"

"Never mind," I said. "You won't have to deal with me anymore! That's what you want! That's what everybody wants!"

I hurried into the garage, bundled up the tent, and ran across the road to a large, wooded state park. It was after 8 pm, and I walked deep into the woods until it got dark. I pitched the tent and noticed the hole in the roof I never got around to fixing. *If it rains, I won't care*, I thought. *I'm gonna die here anyway.* I turned my phone off to save battery and to avoid any signals that might give away my location. I guzzled as much vodka as I could, hoping to not wake up again. This was it – the rock bottom, the end. I *wanted* to die – I *deserved* to die – buried deep in the muddy forest where no one would ever find me.

The flapping sound of the tattered tent woke me in the morning. My eyes slowly opened, and I felt disgustingly sick, depressed, and didn't want to move a muscle. More than anything I was angry I had another day to live in these miserable conditions. I wanted the earth to fold in around me and suck me in. My throat was so parched I couldn't swallow, so I searched for a container to get water. The only thing I had was the vodka bottle, and I wasn't giving that up, even for water. I found a couple of empty beer bottles by a tree and searched for a house at the edge of the park, hoping to spot an outside faucet. I snuck in a backyard, filled the containers, and found my way back to the tent.

A couple more days went by like this, and without food I was getting delirious. I was so tired and weak I was giving up, and began looking for a rope to hang myself from a tree. What stopped me, of all things, was the thought of my mom seeing me with my eyes pecked out by birds after being left in woods for days. With that thought, I turned my phone on and texted mom telling her I was alive. Then I texted a friend who is a cop, and he said everyone was looking for me, and the helicopter was searching too. So, instead of coming out, I hid even deeper in woods.

The hunger and loneliness were too much, and I couldn't take it anymore. I needed food and the only place I knew to get it was my mom's house. When I saw no one was home, I snuck in and ate some fruit and bread. It was all my stomach could handle. Then I "borrowed" my mother's car and headed to Katie's house. I knew she was at work, so I thought I'd get more food and a few of my things.

Upon arrival, I found she changed the locks, but I was determined to find my way in. I tried every door and window, but they were all locked. The garage was open, but not the door into the house. I saw my tool bag on the garage floor, filled with some tools I'd left behind, including a 22-ounce framing hammer, and a couple of Sawzall blades I used to cut drywall. I had often repurposed the blades and made drywall "knives" by making a wood handle and taping it tightly to the other end of the blade.

I was walking back towards the car and suddenly thought about the second-floor slider outside the bedroom. *If I can only get up to the balcony…*, I thought. *Just maybe the slider will be unlocked.*

I dragged the patio table below the deck to stand on, but it was too low. Then I stacked two chairs on top, balanced myself on the arms of the chair, and reached as far as I could. Still a few feet short. I wasn't giving up yet and desperately looked for a way to get up to the deck. Just then, I noticed a Verizon truck at a neighbor's house with a ladder on top. I swear it had my name on it!

I walked to the truck, unhooked the clamps like I owned it, and carried the ladder to my backyard. Yes, "my" backyard – it still belonged to me. I took the tool bag up the ladder with me, just in case I needed to pry open the door. It didn't budge, so I put the hammer to good use. A few forceful whacks on the glass and the door exploded like a bomb. I reached through the opening, unlatched the lock, and slid the door open. I stepped over the glass, threw my tool bag on the bed, and saw the cat run away in fear.

I grabbed some food and was about to leave when I impulsively looked for evidence of the affair I knew Katie was having. I fully expected to find his clothes hanging in my closet. I rummaged through all the closets, drawers, and cabinets, looking for clues. I tore the place apart but found nothing. Then I flipped through her calendar and knew I had her. She circled our divorce day and scribbled "Las Vegas trip" on the very next day.

She couldn't wait one damn day!! It appeared she was planning a getaway trip with her new boyfriend. That *had* to be it. *What now,* I thought. *Screw it, I'll confront her.* I called her at work from her home phone. I made some wild accusations and asked about her trip to Vegas.

"How do you know about that?" she asked.

"I'm looking at your calendar, do you think I'm stupid?" There was a pause, and I realized maybe I *was* stupid after all. She obviously checked the caller ID and saw I was at her house, clearly violating the restraining order.

"You aren't supposed to be there! I'm calling the police!" The heavy click told me I had about two minutes to get the hell out of there.

I crawled back down the ladder and brought it back across the street. No time to re-latch, so I leaned it against the van. I'm sure it gave the Verizon guy something to think about later.

I jumped into the car and drove down the street at a normal speed to avoid any attention. Good move, as several cop cars passed me with their lights flashing on the way to the house. It was then I remembered leaving my open tool bag on Katie's bed, but it was too late to retrieve it. I made it out by 10 seconds!

The drive home should have taken 30 minutes, but it was an hour and a half before I pulled into my mother's driveway.

I can't recall why, or even where I went, but I must have been driving around in a mindless, zombie-like state. I have no recollection of the return trip.

My mom was there when I pulled in and she asked where I'd been. I told her the truth. She said the police called asking about me and she expected them soon. I thought of running out back to the woods but hesitated. My mom and Dan were asking me questions, but my brain couldn't think straight. A loud knock at the door interrupted us and Dan opened the door. It was the police. From the kitchen I heard Dan say, "Oh no, Bart…"

In a panic, I ran out the back door. I didn't get ten feet away before two officers to my right shouted at me to stop. I took one step to the left and saw two more officers with their guns pointed at me. "STOP RIGHT THERE!" they commanded, and instructed me to put my hands up slowly and get down on my knees. Two more officers came from the house, pulled my hands behind my back, and handcuffed me while the guns remained drawn at me. I complied, but one of them kept barking at me to stop resisting. I forcefully shouted back, "I'm not resisting, I am NOT resisting!" I think he was just looking for an excuse to roughen me up.

I didn't understand the extreme treatment I was getting. And my mom had to be wondering what her son could have possibly done to have the police draw out their guns in her back yard. All this for a restraining order violation?

One cop asked, "Why did you come back here?"

"Because it's where I live," I answered. "I have nowhere else to go."

"Well, you're in big trouble now. And you are lucky we got you before you hurt somebody," he added.

I didn't understand what he meant at first, but later found out Katie told the cops she was afraid for her life. When Katie and the police arrived at her house, they found the bedroom door shattered and glass all over the bedroom floor. That, and my open tool bag on her bed – with the six-inch serrated blades resembling "Rambo knives" on top – and concluded I went there intending to kill her. Nothing could be farther from the truth, but it explains why the police seized me the way they did.

Janet: *When I first saw Bart come into the house, I was relieved he was alive. My relief quickly vanished, and I didn't know whether to be angry or fearful. He looked skinny, filthy, and smelled awful. We had barely a minute together before the police arrived, and next thing I know they're shouting, pointing guns, and taking him away in handcuffs. It terrified me. I asked them if I could talk to him, hug him, or just say goodbye and they just told me to stay away and not to touch him. And just like that, they were gone.*

That little stunt landed me back in jail for 3 months. I was miserable, but at least I had food and a bed. My 50th birthday was coming up, and I was on a mission to get drunk to celebrate. So, I learned how to make Pruno, aka prison wine, using a simple distillation process with fruit, water, and bread. It wasn't so easy to get enough ingredients, and even more difficult to avoid detection from the Corrections Officers (CO's). I made a friend in the commissary who got me a few extra apples, and I traded other items for more fruit and Raisin Bran cereal (it worked best for the yeast ingredient). I'd take bites of an apple and spit the soggy, chewed up pieces in a plastic commissary bag, empty peanut butter jar, or shampoo bottle – any tightly sealed container. Then I'd add some raisin bran or white bread, some extra sugar, warm water, and seal it up. A few times a day it needed burping, and when the bloating stopped, the mixture was ready – usually after 3 to 5 days. Pretty gross, but when you're desperate, you're not fussy.

Making Pruno is prohibited, and of course, I got caught. A "random" search was conducted, and they found all my containers – 12 of them – and confiscated everything. They promptly arrested me in my jail cell on my 50th birthday. I found out later they gave my stuff away to people who ratted me out.

They took me to a security room where a bunch of COs, including women, conducted a complete body search. There is nothing more humiliating than standing naked in front of a group of people while being inspected and probed. The video camera pointing at me made it that much better.

I was sentenced to spend a few days in the hole where the waist high steel door meant you had to bend over to accept your food and talk to anyone. It was through this steel door a CO told me I was being charged with possessing contraband. I argued there were no rules against having fruit juice in the cell. "All right," he said. "Have it your way. We'll get you for *conspiring* to obtain contraband."

He laughed and walked away. I had nothing left to say, and just sat on the cement floor with my back against the wall. I've had better birthdays.

Janet: *I didn't understand what was going on with Bart and wasn't entirely sure why he was in jail. We hired a lawyer to get answers and made many trips to court. The visits to jail were traumatizing, and I cried every time Dan and I left. I was afraid Bart would die in jail. He wasn't stable, and not a day would go by where I didn't think I'd get a call with the inevitable fatal news. The lawyer helped us get Bart out with the condition he went through the AISS (After Incarceration Support Services).*

If I stayed in jail another day, I might have killed someone, or myself. I was willing to do anything to get out. From there I gladly went to detox in Fall River for 10 days. I came home on a bus, sober, and ready to start off clean. I got a job at a restaurant and things were moving slowly but steadily.

Janet: *We made an appointment for Bart to see a licensed social worker/therapist, and he spent the night at Baystate Medical Center. From there they sent him to Brookline, MA for a lockdown rehab. The therapist helped Bart get into Providence Hospital Detox, and he came out sober. My husband Dan helped Bart get a job at a restaurant in South Hadley. He did well, but I was cautiously optimistic about Bart giving up drinking. All the countless times over the years prepared me for his next relapse. It wasn't a question of "if," but "when."*

Rebecca (Licensed social worker, LiCSW/therapist): *Upon meeting Bart, I had to ask myself how this intelligent, gregarious, middle-aged guy ended up here with me, instead of a private practice psychologist's office in the suburbs? Was his story embellished to impress me? Was he delusional? Was he having a manic episode with psychosis? This is when it becomes invaluable to have what we in the field call collaterals – people who can verify details and information to get a clearer picture of the person before us. Janet and Dan's input were invaluable to understanding Bart's story and initial treatment needs.*

While going through After Incarceration Support Services program, they also required me to attend AA meetings. I met a woman named Carol there and soon we became friendly. I ignored a basic rule of NOT going out with anyone in detox rehab program, but arrogantly thought I was smarter than most people and could handle anything that came my way.

Rebecca: *Bart now came to therapy excited by the wealth of information and insight he was gaining about addiction and himself. Like any of us, we rely on our strengths, which can be a double-edged sword. Bart's ability to socialize easily, connect with others and assume leadership positions took over, and he started a facebook page for recovering addicts. He also met a young woman, Carol, through AA and they quickly became a couple. Bart was in the early glow of recovery referred to as "the Pink Cloud" where people feel they have found the solution and will never drink/use again. However, as evidenced by Bart's story, it frequently means other suggestions like holding off on getting involved in a romantic relationship for at least a year, or getting a sponsor and working the steps of recovery get overlooked. Bart was slowly taking back control thinking he knew how to manage sobriety. For Bart, it also meant, "Now that I know recovery, I am going to save others." I identified this as a pattern of Bart's stemming from childhood. He was gravitating to what came easy while dismissing the time and effort long-term recovery requires.*

I remained sober for almost two years. Carol, on the other hand, had 5 relapses. Out of three and a half years together, she was away for one hundred and seventy-five days of it. I started a sober program support group and coached many people, including Carol. The coaching helped me as much as the others, but I could not stay strong for long, being surrounded by the drinking and the stress of it all.

Janet: *He told me he met Carol at AA, and both were alcoholics. I knew when he moved in with her it would be a disaster.*

One afternoon I confronted Carol about her continued drinking, we argued, and she stormed out in anger. I briefly thought about my two ex-wives, and the irony of *me* being the one upset by someone else's excessive drinking. I tore the place apart looking for bottles and found them in all the places I used to hide them; closets, underwear drawers, above ceiling tiles, and even inside the toilet tank. I found 30 bottles of all sizes and laid them out on the bed. I took a picture and sent to her. I was angry, but that wasn't enough, so I had a better idea.

"I'll show her what it's like to see someone relapse!" I said out loud to no one there, while reaching for the bottle of vodka. I sent a selfie video of me drinking large swills right from the bottle. "See what it feels like!!" I shouted at the camera between gulps. "Are you happy?" I didn't care, even if it cost me my life. It was an intentional relapse, and maybe deep down I was looking for a reason to start again. Well, I found one, and of course, blamed her for it.

Carol came home after a few hours and found me out cold. She woke me and I jumped in the shower to sober up. In the shower, I had another seizure. I remember little about it, but the paramedics came when I was naked on the floor and still wet from the shower.

I got home from the hospital and started drinking again. *Why not?* Carol tried stopping me and we'd fight until we lost the energy to continue. The next morning we'd pretend nothing happened and went about our days and weeks and months of hazy, drunken nights, and hungover mornings.

One day we were driving to Maine and while on the Mass Pike we got into a fierce argument. I sped up to over 120 miles per hour and tried to control the car while we were shouting at each other. Carol battered my arm and head while I drove erratically at high speeds endangering other drivers. When we finally arrived at the hotel, we settled down, had a drink, and laughed it off.

"That was crazy, huh?" Carol said, emphasizing crazy.

"Yeah, I could've killed someone," I said. "We went way over a hundred!"

"Oh at least, and I'll bet we scared a few people on the highway," she said laughing. "But the good news is we got here quicker!"

We had a great weekend. No problem at all. This behavior went on with extreme highs and lows that could change in an instant, like a bipolar relationship.

In late February, our landlord gave us a notice to move out by the end of March because he planned to do rehab to the apartment. We started looking for another place to live, when out of the blue, Carol came by with six guys and grabbed all her stuff. She told me it was over, said she'd had enough, and left me hanging with no place to go. A few days later, I was informed she had filed a restraining order.

Janet: *Bart stayed in the apartment until the end of the month and moved back in with me and Dan on April 1. He denied he was drinking, but his erratic behavior told me differently. Everyone knew it, but he still thought he fooled us all. He wasn't eating, drank only milk and vodka, lost a ton of weight, and became freakishly obsessed with exercise. I thought he was having a psychotic breakdown. We exhausted all efforts and had no idea what to do.*

Rebecca: *Bart's mom called saying he was pacing around the house, not showering or eating and his behavior was increasingly strange. He came on the phone and I said it wasn't fair to his parents to continue to put them through this and he needed help. At this point, he surrendered to the idea of going to detox.*

After moving back in with my mom I was eager to get on with my life after detox. My super-wound-up personality didn't allow me to do anything in moderation though. No halfway with me — it's all in or nothing. I didn't know any other way. I'd become obsessed with anything I fixed my mind to do, whether it was a relationship, drinking, or working out. I was on a mission to prove something, and I'd take it to the extreme.

This was the same intensity I brought to my career success, but it came with a heavy price. It took me a long time to realize this personality trait did not serve me well.

A former co-worker named Diane and I became reacquainted through Facebook. I had not seen Diane in over twenty years, but our on-line conversations quickly advanced to more personal topics. She confessed she wanted to have a child before it was too late and asked if I'd be willing to be a voluntary contributor. I'm not sure if it was my damaged self-esteem, or the recent break-up, or my two broken families, or my reckless drinking, or all those things combined that inspired me, but when she asked this incredibly important question, I said, "Sure, why the hell not?" This conversation took place by phone before we met in person. Family planning at its finest.

We set a date for me to go over and "contribute." I arrived at her apartment for dinner and within seconds the warning signals flashed loud and clear. She appeared much different from what I remembered, with dyed hair, tattoos, and piercings I couldn't peel my eyes from. The excessive hoarding was also concerning, as I carefully guided myself through the clutter. I'm a bit OCD, and even with my prison experience, I cringed at the filth. But the good news is the drinking helped me get past all that. And drink we did, in between the multiple attempts to spawn a child.

I had no reason to leave – remember; I had nothing – so I moved in with her. We quickly moved on from trying to conceive a child to "falling in love" to deciding to get married. We purchased rings and filed for a marriage license. Why do anything halfway?

As we got to know each other, she casually mentioned she was part of a gang, one known for its violence. She revealed thirteen bumps on her arm, slightly concealed by tattoos. "Blood in / Blood out" is how she referred to the marks. I questioned what she meant, and she simply said they were healed wounds, a "badge of honor" that represented bodies she was directly responsible for.

"Directly?" I asked. "What do you mean?"

She looked at me like I was stupid and said, "Do I really need to explain that?"

Not wanting to appear ignorant, I shrugged and said, "Hmmm... ok then," followed by, "What do you want for dinner?" I poured some vodka, and we moved on to other things.

We continued to drink heavily, day after day, and her behavior became increasingly wild, even by my own warped observations. If I was the more rational one in this relationship, well then, how bad could things possibly get? We'd fight, she'd start punching me, then we'd make up and end up in bed. Do you see a pattern here? I didn't. I was so impaired and delusional, I saw nothing wrong with this repeated behavior.

One night, in the middle of a deep sleep, she impulsively screamed, "Get out! Get out!!" while hitting me in the face. I tried to block the blows and shouted back, "Alright, alright, I'm leaving." My ear was bleeding, but I threw on my jeans and a tee shirt and headed for the door. She blocked the doorway with her body, said she was sorry and begged me to stay. "Ok, Ok," I said. "I won't leave." We went back to bed like nothing happened. The next morning Diane vowed to stop drinking, while insisting it was interfering with her ability to get pregnant.

With Diane, any minor thing could produce an outburst. One night I made a joke about the Buffalo Bills just to bust her ass, since she was a fan of the team. I mentioned how pathetic it was that they lost four super bowls in a row. This occurred three decades ago, but she was still quite sensitive about it. I kept it up. She got pissed, and it soon escalated out of control. She screamed and threatened to kill me. Even in my slightly drunken state, I wasn't prepared for such an overreaction. I gave her some space and stepped outside. A few minutes later I walked back in and we both apologized, kissed, and hugged.

Then, in a composed, soft voice, she asked me to leave the room for a minute. I agreed but asked why. She said she had to put the gun away.

"The *gun?*" I asked. "*What* gun?"

"Oh, just the 38. The 9 is still locked up."

"Huh?" Silent seconds followed, while Diane's glare said, *Did you hear me?*

I wanted to say *You're a crazy lunatic bitch!* Instead, I said "Ok," without further ado. I left the room and went outside to have a cigarette. A few minutes later, I cautiously knocked on the door.

"All set. It's ok to come in," she said sweetly, as if she'd just put on her prettiest dress.

"Cool."

I walked in, got under the covers and we snuggled in bed like nothing unusual happened. Another day behind us. One thing changed though – I started sleeping with a knife under the bed. Just a small precaution. I couldn't wait to see what the next day would bring.

During this relationship, I could have walked away at any time. Part of me recognized the madness I was deeply involved in, and another part didn't care. I was reduced to this crazy life by my own choices, but I accepted and allowed it because it was all I had. Nothing else, and no one else, mattered anymore anyway.

Although my previous relationship with Carol had been over for several months, one of her friends felt a lingering need to protect her from me and continued to harass me. I tried to ignore him, but when he physically threatened my mother, he went over the line.

We arranged to meet and fight it out. The one rule was fists only – no weapons. He said he'd bring someone just to make sure he didn't get ambushed. I said I would too. Here I was at 53 years old ready to fight someone 30 years younger in a dark parking lot, and instead of being nervous, I was excited about it. It is often said that nervousness is a sign of intelligence, and clearly, I had neither.

I told Diane where I was going, and she said she would come along.

"I'll watch your back," she said confidently.

"Whatever, suit yourself," I said. "Let's go."

When we were leaving the house, Diane said she still needed a few minutes to get ready. I primed myself by taking a few healthy swigs from the vodka bottle. She came out of her room with a bag and other items stuffed in her belt.

"Ok, I'm ready," she said.

"What's all this?" I asked.

She went through the inventory as calmly as reading a grocery list.

"First, I have a dog choke chain to take him down from behind. And superglue to squirt in his eyes."

"Wait," I said. "We agreed no weapons, just — "

She ignored me and continued. "These shoes have razor blades in the toe, and this is a bottle of garden lye to pour in his mouth, and this..." She paused, patted her hip to emphasize her point, and continued, "*This* is the 38. Just in case."

She made me stop and think about this whole affair differently. So, I grabbed the 10-inch knife from under the mattress and concealed it under my shirt in the small of my back. So much for "fists only." We arrived prepared for war and waited. He never showed up. Disappointed, we went back home, drank, and went to bed.

We hadn't discussed the event for a few weeks until one night while making dinner. Out of the blue, she says, "Hey, remember when we went to kill that boy?"

"Yeah, I remember," I said, nodding. "But I don't care about him anymore."

"Well, he wouldn't have made it out alive."

"Yeah, I know," I said. "He's lucky." Another pull of vodka and another drunken night followed. It never came up again. We continued our routine of drinking, arguing, and fighting. Either one of us would spiral into a rage, usually over trivial matters – with even less importance than the Buffalo Bills – and it was exhausting. The problems only got worse.

I had a warrant out for my arrest for violating a restraining order against Carol. Diane had known this and after one more enraged moment she called the police and told them I was there. She hid my car keys, so I had no escape. I calmly sat in the kitchen and waited in my pajamas for the police to arrive. I was upset, but had no energy to resist, so I cooperated. They took me away in my pajamas to the Hampden County Jail in Ludlow. No hearing, no trial, no bail. Sixty days in the slammer.

Janet: *I received a call that Bart was taken to the Ludlow jail. I had mixed feelings because honestly, I didn't know if he was safer in jail or with Diane. We visited Bart, but this time it was different. The facility was an upgrade from Hartford, slightly less stark and depressing, but it was still a jail. Bart appeared defeated, as if he was giving up. His ego, protective wall, and bullet proof attitude had broken down, and he was an empty shell of himself. Somehow, this change scared me more than anything. I felt like I was watching him die slowly and couldn't do a thing about it.*

The relationship with Diane ended with my incarceration. Thank God for that. As I lay in my cell and stared at the ceiling, I reflected on what my life had become. I had lacked any direction, and rather than set my course, I had reacted to the madness around me and instinctively adapted to my new surroundings. Problems were being solved through my severely poisoned and distorted brain, yet underneath it all I was still the same person with a sense of honesty and morals and integrity. Any remnants of who I was had been drowned out by alcohol.

I thought about how I ruined my first marriage, and when offered a second chance at a happy family, I destroyed that too. I had the world in the palm of my hands and threw it all away, not once but twice. How did I go from sipping fine wine at Tanglewood concerts to slugging warm vodka from a bottle in a dirty kitchen planning a murder?

All I had left were hazy memories of drunken nights, evading police, wildly stressful relationships, and of course, the misery of living in a jail cell. Darkness, sickness, despair, and loneliness were all I had to look forward to, and I only had myself to blame. I no longer recognized who I was and hated who I saw in the mirror. I had wasted my entire life, burned every relationship, and had nothing but self-inflicted wreckage to show for it. At my age there were no second chances, no do-overs, and with this depressing thought, an immense sadness weighed me down. I wondered, *Do I have anything left in me to change? Is it possible to salvage any part of my past I had destroyed?* If so, I had choices to make, and my life depended on it.

The following day a fellow inmate approached me and asked if I would like to attend a bible study meeting. I laughed and told him he was asking the wrong guy.

"Why not come along?" he asked. "It can't hurt."

"Because I'm an atheist, that's why!" I replied, hoping he'd go away.

"Are you happy being an atheist?" he calmly persisted.

"Yes… no, I mean…, I'm not happy being anything." I rambled, "It has nothing to do with that, it's just…" I couldn't articulate an answer as he forced me to think about something I hadn't thought about for over thirty years.

"You have more important things to do while sitting here?" he sarcastically interrupted.

"No, I don't." He had me there. I reluctantly agreed to go.

Now, I will admit, when I walked into the bible study, I tightened up and told myself I didn't need the bible. No more than I needed detox, or rehab, or AA, or a counselor. I was powerful enough on my own. And yet, there I was in jail again, right where my own selfish ego led me. If my way was working out so well, why the hell was I here? I sat down, listened, and observed something happening in front of me. These were convicts, living in miserable conditions, and I didn't see anger among them, but joy instead. I saw hope, not despair. The selfishness I'd been accustomed to around me was absent, and replaced with modesty, humility, and genuine care for each other.

A wave of emotion overwhelmed me so much I cannot adequately describe it. For the first time in decades, I let my defenses down and allowed myself to surrender. I know it sounds like a cliché, but the Holy Spirit entered me, and I felt it. My new friend came over, put his hand on my shoulder and said, "Many of us have found Christ in jail." He asked if I'd like to pray with him, and we did. As if he knew, we prayed for forgiveness of our enemies, and a complete surrender to the will of God. I continued to attend bible study and attended church services in jail. My time in Hampden County Jail in Ludlow lasted sixty days.

When I came back home, an old friend reached out to me. She knew my troubled history and current situation, and she asked if I'd like to visit her church. I asked a few questions and agreed to go. I told her I was saved in jail, confessed I had a long way to go and wanted to learn more. While attending one of the services I learned about Celebrate Recovery, a Christian program for people dealing with addiction. I liked what I heard, met with a few counselors and former addicts, and joined the program. It was the best decision I have ever made. The support I've had from the church, the counselors, and new friends has been tremendous, and thanks to all of them, I am no longer living in darkness. I have a lot of work to do, but I am not looking back – only forward.

Rebecca: *I referred Bart to a family therapist to guide him through the potential loss of relationship with his children. Bart believed if he saw his son Matthew, he could repair their relationship, but I encouraged him to resist the desire to force reconciliation. So much harm had been done to Matthew, it had to be left to Matthew, not Bart. Often the instinctual need for re-affiliation and forgiveness from family can overrun the person in early recovery and lead to more resentment and distance from loved ones harmed. As in the case with Bart, his son did not want reconciliation. It is important to stress to the recovering person in this situation, the story is not over. It means not now, and no one knows how things may change in the future. With sobriety, all things remain possible.*

If there was one thing I learned from my 11 years as a home remodeler, it is that you cannot build something new over old broken-down structures or a weakened foundation. Rooms had to be "gutted," and the more neglected and abused, the more difficult the demolition. Only after destroying and removing the damaged goods can you rebuild something beautiful. I've learned these same principals apply to our lives. You need to do a complete demolition of ego, arrogance, and ugly baggage first. And remove the people, places, and things from your past life to build anew. I believe God had to break me before rebuilding. I have also learned to fix *me* first. I will be no good to anyone unless I am strong and sober. I now have a future with a purpose, and I am dedicating myself to helping others get through addictions and salvage their lives before it is too late.

I have not talked with my daughters in over fifteen years. And over ten years for my son Matthew. Every day I wake up hoping and praying with everything I have that my children will accept me someday soon, not as the man I was, but the man I have become. Each day brings me closer.

Clinician's comments

Bart returned to therapy after his second incarceration. He came back in much the same physical and mental shape as before. We see the progressive nature of addiction, which over time takes the afflicted person to darker places and lowers the capacity for rational decision making. Bart drank again after jail and needed detox. When he left my office, it was his job to call daily to get a bed when one opened. Bart followed through, and when he returned to therapy, he was ready to look at past his trauma, something he hadn't been able to do before.

Bart completed a Cognitive Behavioral Evidenced Based 12-week therapy for trauma called CPT or Cognitive Processing Therapy for PTSD. This therapy looks at how exposure to trauma can challenge a person's belief system leading to the development of irrational beliefs and behavior. These dysfunctional patterns occur in repeating cycles and only bring more pain and disconnection. CPT helps to challenge these irrational beliefs and interrupt dysfunctional patterns, allowing healthier ones to emerge.

This combined with Bart finding a program of recovery, and the recognition he benefits from medication for depression, is offering him another chance to live a whole full life. Not as the same Bart we met at the beginning of his story, but as the Bart he is coming to know in the present. A person who does not have to lead, fix, or be the best at anything but himself.

Questions and discussion points

Bart had a tendency to do things to an extreme. How much did that contribute to his drinking?

Bart's mom Janet said, *"When Bart is sober, he is a thoughtful, intelligent, caring person. Drinking changes all that."* Perhaps you recognize some of Bart's personality traits in others? Or yourself?

Does it change when influenced by alcohol?

Bart's path to recovery was one he did not expect and was initially reluctant to try.

It may not be right for everyone, but if nothing else is working for someone you love, their recovery may have a better chance at success.

THE LITTLE DEVIL MAN

Sterling

The piercing cold stabbed me like steel icicles shooting through my veins. Lying there paralyzed, I didn't know what was happening. Just seconds before, a calming warmth flowed into my blood the instant the syringe was pressed. My eyes fell shut and my body filled with a sense of relief, and for a moment, I was going to that wonderful place I found the first time I used heroin. That was always the moment I liked best – anticipating the ecstasy, watching it enter my body. But instead, it deceived me, and the feeling went from numb to terrifyingly cold. My body quivered uncontrollably, and I closed my eyes, hoping for it all to end. The sharp biting pain wouldn't go away, and I thought I had died. It was the last thing I remembered.

When my eyes sluggishly opened, I realized I couldn't be dead, but was unsure if it was a good thing or not. My entire body was numb and didn't know how much time passed. Shrouded in darkness, I sat up, feeling deeply ashamed for what I had become. I used to be the strong and muscular one who challenged all my friends. Now, my six-foot two body was a lifeless shell of what it once was, depleted of strength, and nothing but a pathetic self-pitying carcass. My face was drawn and pale, eyes vacant. Feeling needy and helpless as a newborn baby, all I wanted to do was curl up in a fetal position and forget I existed.

Through the darkness I heard the voices of my friends Jeff and Cara. They had been with me in the park where we all flock to use heroin with no interfering cops. Jeff and Cara walked by, at first ignoring me. Maybe I really didn't exist after all, and it was ok with me. But then Jeff turned and kicked me in the side and said, "Come on Sterling, let's get the hell out of here." Well, that was a helluva *"Welcome back, my friend"* greeting to wake up to. With that kick, I felt even more unwanted and worthless. Cara laughed and said, "Maybe we can get some more sweet thing tonight". I knew she meant heroin, and she thought I could help them get more. That's what my life was worth to them. I had no place else to go, so I followed them.

I trailed them up the hill to the city streets, the same streets where I panhandled just hours before. Yes, me, the strong carpenter who once owned a sixty-thousand-dollar truck, lost it all to the drug, and now I had to panhandle to buy the thing that destroyed me. All I could think of was, *How did my life become this meaningless empty void?*

Jeff and Cara walked ahead of me, speaking to each other, as I fell behind and reminisced. Memories of living with Lina and her family flooded my mind, and how much I missed the warmth of her home and the smell of dinner cooking. I "adopted" Lina as my mother when I was nineteen, because she was full of love and cared about me like her own son.

We'd sit around the dinner table laughing and talking about the day's events. Her own children Nicki, Natalie, and Jay treated me like a brother, and we'd often go fishing, camping, and drinking with their friends. My brain, even in its diminished capacity, kept asking, *When did all this become not enough? Why did I trade it all away for a few selfish minutes of hazy oblivion?* These questions pounded at my brain like a hammer and wouldn't stop. Lina had taken me into her home under one condition – I would never use heroin again. I failed miserably when I broke that promise to her. Heroin consumed me at the expense of everything I had, and I constantly craved for more, night and day. What used to be important just didn't matter anymore; no hunger for food, no thirst for water - if I could trade the air I breathe for heroin I would have. I felt nothing at all, except for the driving need to use heroin. I ruined it all and there was no way they would take me back. I was ashamed of who I was, and regretful of who I was not.

Lina: *My God, did I miss Sterling. We had so much fun when he was around. He slipped into this family as a needy older brother, looking for love from all of us. He thrived when he was with us at the dinner table, laughing about his latest antics. Even fishing with him was different. He would start singing "Fishing with Sterling" and then tried to teach us what to do. Then he made us laugh when he fell into the water. His energy was like an over excited two-year-old. He was larger than life and wanted to always have more... more food, more laughs, more fishing, more camping, more booze..., but what he wanted most was more belonging. He wanted everyone to like him, but he didn't always know how to do it. He could be overwhelming, and people would push him away. Like when he would tell my daughter Natalie, "You know you love me."*

Natalie once told him he did not have any social skills. He argued that he knew how to smoke pot with friends. She told him that didn't count. I will never forget how Sterling came to me like a hurt child asking me to tell him he really did have social skills. Of course, I told him he did, but it was when he was charming and fun, not when he smoked pot. I enjoyed being Sterling's mother. I thought he would be with me for the rest of my time on this earth. He belonged to me. I wanted to do everything I could to make him happy, as I did my other children. I often wondered, "How did I fail him?"

I thought about Nicki, Lina's daughter, my best friend, who I loved dearly, and realized she would never have me this way. I didn't blame her. She wanted more and deserved more than I could give her. I tried to hide my addiction from her, but she knew much more than she let on. She saw the needle marks on my arm, and I told her it was a cigarette burn. *Did I really think I was fooling her? Or anyone else?* After that, I started shooting between my toes, but Nicki saw the change in me. We had so much fun together drinking and partying, but she never crossed that line I crossed, that line I thought I could come back from. Nicki said she wouldn't talk to me until I got clean. *So, ok,* I thought, *I'll just have to live without my best friend.* That's all there was to it. I missed her, but not as much as I'd miss the drug. I had different friends now, and a new girlfriend, Mindy. I didn't have to hide anything or lie to her. No resistance, and no questioning. I liked it that way.

Mindy shot up with me and didn't think this lifestyle was so bad. She was pretty, but I noticed her appearance and personal hygiene changing. I wondered if she noticed the same about me. I didn't really care anyway. I didn't even want sex any more the way I used to. Our routine was to pass out together at night and then go back to the streets in the morning.

I followed Jeff and Cara to a spot downtown where we thought we could find some heroin. I saw Mindy on the corner walk off with a couple of guys and should've been jealous, but I honestly didn't care. I never asked what she did, because she usually came home with cash, or had a stash of drugs on her. Heroin was our drug of choice, but we'd take whatever we got our hands on. We made an excellent team, Mindy and I, and one of us was always bringing home the goods. Being with her made me feel valuable and needed.

When I got back to my apartment that night without scoring again, the two men I saw Mindy with were walking down the stairs. One of them high-fived me and said, "Nice girlfriend." *Hmm,* I thought, *I wonder what he meant by that?* When I came through the door Mindy said, "Look what I got," and showed me the heroin. Suddenly, the stairway comments were unimportant. It was three days before we left the apartment.

Weeks later, Nicki and Lina came to take me to lunch for my 29th birthday. Around 11 am they found me with my new friends in front of the First Church where we hung out. My friends scattered when they saw them coming towards me. Lina smiled and asked how I was, but she had a sadness in her eyes. Nicki was still upset with me, and the first thing she did was check my arms for needle marks and then she opened my backpack. I was scared she'd find my stuff. I had a needle in an eyeglass case and maybe a bag of heroin, if I didn't already use it – I couldn't remember. Nicki peered into my bag and said, "Never mind. I don't want to know." I breathed a sigh of relief and so did Lina.

We walked across the street to a small lunch restaurant, but I had no appetite. I ate half my sandwich and put the other half in my backpack without thinking. Lina frowned and asked what was wrong. I didn't want to upset her, so I lied and told her I had a late breakfast. I was afraid Lina and Nicki saw I had become an empty shell of a person who could no longer make them laugh. Nicki barely said a word the whole time. I knew I had to get out of there before disappointing them more, so I lied again and told them I had a job interview. I just stacked one lie upon another, promising I would call at least once a week. The lunch left me feeling even more hollow than before, and I started craving the drug right before their eyes. It wasn't a sandwich I wanted. It wasn't the peace and contentment of being loved by people I loved. It was the damn heroin I needed quickly. Even though I missed the life with them, the drug was more powerful. I don't remember the rest of my 29th birthday.

Lina: *I was so excited. Nicki and I had a date to meet Sterling for his birthday. It was going to be a great day. Sterling loved to eat, so I was going to take him to his restaurant of choice and let him order whatever he wanted. I was looking forward to his childlike excitement when he enjoyed a meal and maybe a few drinks. Since we hadn't seen* *each other for a while, I looked forward to spending hours with him laughing, talking, and walking. He always had so much energy. I was sure he would want to walk to the park, maybe even run in the park.*

When we first arrived, I didn't see Sterling at our meeting spot. Then Nicki pointed at him across the street. There he was, standing with his backpack on his back like a nervous little boy waiting for his first day of kindergarten. I noticed his hair was longer than usual, but it was not the spiked blue mohawk he once cherished. His hair hung there, limp against his neck. This was a look I had never seen before on Sterling. He smiled at us, but his smile lacked the mischievous charm I once saw every single day. Who was this person?

I thought maybe he would perk up once we were at the restaurant. To my surprise, he only wanted to go the sandwich shop across the street. He ordered a sandwich, but he didn't even finish it. I didn't know what to think anymore. It was if the Sterling we knew was fading away right before our eyes, and we could no longer penetrate the wall around him. Still, I thought I would have many more chances to see Sterling and help him find his way. I slipped him some money when Nicki wasn't looking. She would have been mad at me because she insisted he was using heroin. I didn't want to believe it, but something wasn't right. I still thought he would come home someday and put this all behind him. After all, this was just a phase. Yet, when he left us that day, I remember turning around and seeing him disappear into the crowd as if he were no longer mine. I felt a sense of ambiguous loss that day.

It had been about two years since I moved to this city. The first year I lived on the streets and would sleep in the little tent city by the park. It's where I learned to panhandle. I couldn't sleep in the tent city unless I paid a guy named Bill twenty bucks a week. Bill sort of ran things around the tent city. He threw me out the first night and I slept on the bench in front of First Church. I met Jeff there and he showed me how to panhandle. I found my spot over by the highway where people coming home from work had to stop at the red light. There were days I made 70 bucks and shared some with Jeff and his girlfriend.

Cara wasn't Jeff's girlfriend at the time, Betsy was. Betsy overdosed six months ago in Shepard's Park. Jeff and I tried to wake her by throwing cold soda in her face, but nothing worked. By the time the ambulance came, it was too late. She didn't look dead to me, lying there peacefully with a smile on her face. I wondered if she slipped into the warm embrace of the drug like the feeling of that first high, just before she died. When the ambulance and police came, our instincts told us to lie and protect ourselves, so we told the police she went off and used on her own and we weren't using. They knew it wasn't true, but what could they do? All I knew then was I would not end up like Betsy. I *knew* how much heroin to use.

A mere two weeks later, Jeff had a new girlfriend, Cara. That's how easily we could detach emotionally, avoiding any meaningful connection. Move on, do more drugs, disregard all else. The only relationships that mattered were those enabling us to use drugs. Others were merely an impediment. Things were much easier this way.

At first, living in the tent city was the greatest thing. My new friends understood me, accepted my drug use without questioning, and brought me into their circle. For a brief time, I felt I belonged, but I was kidding myself. There was no loyalty, no friendship, no love. Nothing at all like being with Lina and her family where there was genuine concern, honesty, and unconditional love.

The drug community "friends" were all on a self-serving mission motivated by the singular goal of getting high. People would help me if it meant helping themselves. We had it all figured out though; how to get money we needed, where to get drugs, which church had free food, how to get a free bus pass, and how to get warm clothes from the Salvation Army. Then the winter would come, and the drug wasn't even enough to keep me warm. I hated sleeping out in the cold. The tents didn't hold up much when the wind blew, especially at below zero temperatures. I did not want to spend another winter in the cold and was thrilled one day when my social worker said she'd help me find an apartment. She told me she had called Lina to find out where I was. I had previously given her Lina's number as my next of kin. So, when I called Lina and told her about my apartment, I also told her I was doing fantastic. Saying anything else might prompt questions I wasn't willing to answer, and I didn't want her to be disappointed. I could tell she was happy for me and spoke with a sense of renewed hope.

Lina: I remember thinking Sterling was finally going to be okay. After all, I set him up with a social worker who was going to find him permanent housing and a mental health provider who would make sure he took his meds. His social worker also got him health insurance, food stamps, and a phone. I thought he was finally getting settled, but then he stopped answering his phone. His social worker called to ask where he was, and I told her I didn't know.

I drove around the streets near the college where he was supposed to be living and sat on a park bench to wait for him. I saw so many unfamiliar faces, but no Sterling. Several more days passed, and I never saw him. Fall was upon us and it was getting cold. Nicki and I walked through the college and asked for Sterling by name, hoping someone would be kind enough to tell us something. It was getting colder by the minute when we stopped a young man Sterling's age and asked if he had seen him. Finally, instead of brushing us off, he told us to wait at the bus stop on the side street a few blocks away. I couldn't help wondering if we had missed Sterling all those previous times by just a few blocks.

We had no idea if the young man was telling us the truth, but we checked it out. After the third bus we were ready to give up, then a fourth bus pulled up and out came Sterling with a young woman we had never met. We were uncertain of what to expect, but Nicki toughened up and asked where he had been. Sterling laughed and sat down. He introduced us to his girlfriend, but she mumbled something and disappeared in a moment. We were too busy staring at Sterling to notice her. He looked paler and even thinner than the last time we saw him. His vibrancy had faded even more.

Nicki and I sat with Sterling and talked for close to an hour. I told him he needed to call his social worker to keep his benefits. He said he would. He showed us his "new" coat from the Salvation Army and said he was all set for the cold weather. He told us life was FANTASTIC, with a little too much emphasis to be believed, and that he and his girlfriend had a new apartment. "What else could I possibly need?" he asked. We spent the time laughing about the past, and Sterling told us stories about the people walking by. He was getting edgy, and I thought he just wanted to catch up with his girlfriend. We came to see how he was doing, and seeing he was ok, we let him go with a few hugs, kisses. He made a few more promises we were skeptical of. I watched as he walked back towards his girlfriend with a slow posture of defeat.

Sterling was willing to give us some time that day, but not willing to share his life with us. He was not the same person, and he didn't want us to know who he'd become. There was a cold unease about him, and he drifted in and out when he spoke. He would laugh with us and then stare into space as if we didn't exist. He appeared as if he needed to be somewhere else, with someone else, doing something else. His stare was one of longing. A longing of something we could not give him. I wasn't sure then, but I am now, that Sterling wanted us to

hold on to the vision of the man he once was. He was giving
us permission to be in denial, and we so easily took it.

It wasn't long after I got my apartment when I met Mindy on the bus, and she moved in with me. She didn't want to live in the tent city because she said there were too many perverts there. They were some people who didn't use heroin who ran the place, like Bill, who made money off the heroin users. Others would steal our stuff or take advantage of the girls when they passed out. Mindy didn't belong there and needed to stay with me. It was good to have someone to talk to, to hang with, and to use with. Mindy didn't ask questions, and she didn't judge me when I showed fear from my demons. She just told me it would be alright.

I used heroin because of those demons. I started seeing them in high school and my friends laughed at me and didn't want to hang with me because I scared them. At first, they thought I was kidding, but I just got too weird for them. I actually dealt with what I called "the little devil man" since I was five years old after I nearly drowned. He teased me all my life, but it was when the full-size creatures came and started talking to me, I had to find a way out. At first alcohol and pot was enough, and I just wanted to fit in and belong, so I became a drunk and a pothead. They thought I was the cool one without a care in the world. How wrong they were.

I wasn't diagnosed with schizophrenia until I was in prison for selling heroin a few years before. I was running around the place naked yelling the devil was going to get me. They put me in the infirmary and the psychiatrist medicated me. The medication made me feel normal for the first time in my adult life. I couldn't wait to get out of there and live straight like other people. Unfortunately, the first thing I did when I got out was go straight to a bar and drink. For an awfully long time afterwards it seemed that drinking was the only way I could keep a group of friends. Then Lina took me in, and there were other things to live for.

I had a new family, a job, a place to come home to after work, dinner on the table, and my best friend, Nicki. For years this worked. I still drank and smoked weed, but I went to work and had a home where I belonged. Then everyone started growing up and moving on. I just couldn't find my place in life and found my way back to heroin. It tripped me up once again. At first, it calmed my hallucinations so much better than anything the doctor ever gave me

On the morning of April 7th. I awoke early and felt sick. The heroin wasn't doing much anymore, other than making me feel just ok. I had to take it, or I would start getting violently sick. The little devil man would come out and say, *"Take the stuff or you'll die"*. I hated the little devil man and didn't want to see him anymore. Maybe I *wanted* to die. At least I wouldn't feel the pain of living anymore. When I was a child, my family didn't understand me, and when I was a teenager, my friends didn't understand me. I had a new family who understood me for a short while, but somehow it wasn't enough, and it was time to go. I didn't want them to suffer knowing I betrayed their trust.

I spent my entire life searching for the place I belonged, and suddenly I realized the drug addict life wasn't it. It was pretend – all a lie. The drug tricked my brain into thinking nothing else mattered but getting high. I decided then I was going to get clean. I was going to heal my brain and my body. So easy to say. *But how?* I could go back to drinking for a while until I got this drug out of my system. That was my plan. I didn't think I could do it alone, so I went down to the package store and bought a bottle of vodka. I was halfway through the bottle when I decided to call all the people who I loved. I wanted them to know I was coming back. I first called my father, and he said to me, "I told you not to call me when your high or drunk." And he hung up.

That didn't stop me. I called a few old friends and talked about the good old days. I saved the best for last. I called Lina's house to talk with Nicki, Natalie, and Jay. Only Lina was home, and she was getting ready for work. She said she wanted to see me Saturday and asked me to meet her at the same restaurant we had lunch in front of the First Church. We talked about the time she took me to the beach for a week with Natalie to help her get over a breakup. She said she would take us again. We had a plan for the future. I told her I would do anything for her and her daughters, and said they meant the world to me. Lina responded by saying, "I know Sterling. I love you too." She had to go, but she made me promise I would be there on Saturday in front of the church. I was disappointed Nicki wasn't there to speak with, but I went right back to my vodka.

I staggered out of the apartment and got on the bus to go to downtown to tell my friends the good news. I would not use anymore. I sat there on the bench in the damp, drizzly day and wondered where everybody went. An eerie feeling came over me and I feared the little devil man was coming, but I was still too drunk to feel him. Then I saw Jeff standing across the street, leaning against the corner of the building. I could barely see his face, but knew it was him by his purple ski hat. He wasn't alone and appeared to be pulling Cara towards him and kissing her. I walked towards them, and suddenly Jeff pushed her away and I saw it wasn't Cara. It was Mindy. I was still unsteady on my feet but knew what I saw. Jeff smiled and said, "Hey man, I was just helping her through a rough morning". I didn't remember when Mindy left the apartment in the morning, or if she even came home that night. I hadn't a clue.

Mindy just looked at me and said, "I know something special. Follow me." I was too drunk to react or think too much, so I complied. We walked through a few streets to the area of old houses where rooms were rented out and we turned onto the sidewalk of one of the homes. The two of us walked into a filthy apartment that smelled of trash and cats. I felt a tinge of the uneasiness that came before the craving and thought I better get more vodka. There were two people sitting at the kitchen table nodding off. I knew they were in the throes of a heroin high. They didn't care about the trash and smell of old putrid cat litter all around them. Seeing them triggered me to want to be where they were in their minds. I fought off the temptation for the moment. Mindy asked them a question, and one of them pointed to the back room. Mindy went back and returned saying, "We have to come back at five." We left the place and walked back downtown, where we met up with Jeff.

Jeff turned to me and said, "We only have enough left for me and Mindy. We'll go back at five for the good stuff."

I frowned and asked, "Hey man, where's Cara." Jeff shrugged and said, "She went home." I stood there confused as they both walked away laughing. I turned to go to the package store and realized I never told them I wasn't going to use anymore. I spent the rest of the day on the bench drinking. It got dark when I began walking towards the bus stop. I felt sick to my stomach, my head was spinning, and I just wanted to go home. I needed something, and it *wasn't* more vodka. I thought about going to the hospital to tell them how sick I was, with the thought that they could help me get into rehab again. After each rehab, I'd stay clean for a short while until heroin called again. Thirty days of rehab was never enough, no matter how many times I went.

Walking to the bus stop, my veins pounded with pain, as if they were about to explode through my skin. And then, my great antagonizer, the little devil man, came out. He was going to tell me what to do.

I was too weak to fight him. The vodka had weakened my mind, and I had no fight left in me. The little devil man sneered at me and said, *"Who are you kidding? You can't beat me."* I was afraid for my life, so terrified of what he would tell me to do next. Then I saw Jeff and Mindy coming out of the side street we took earlier. I stopped for a moment, turned away from the bus stop, and walked toward them. That turned out to be a poor decision.

There was a third person with them I've never seen before. He looked like he just graduated from high school and acted like a little punk. He looked at me and asked, "You got the cash?" Jeff turned and explained he and Mindy were down at the park all day and forgot to panhandle. He knew I scored big yesterday and still had most of the money. The punk continued, "Give it up man, this stuff is good. It's got fent in it. It'll be like your first high." I didn't know what fent was, but I knew I wanted a good high, and the little devil man gone. He was still sneering at me, taunting me, and I wanted the heroin badly. I threw twenty bucks at the little punk and he handed Jeff the stash of heroin.

Despite all I had promised myself, there I was with the needle in my arm. *Tomorrow*, I thought, *I will start over.* I even said it out loud to drive it home: *Tomorrow I will re-train my brain. I will find my way back to who I was and the people I loved and who really loved me. I will never use again after today. Tomorrow I will deal with my demons, the pain of dope sickness, the pain of the little devil man antagonizing me, and the pain of my failure. It all had to go away. Tomorrow. Right now*, I thought, *I have an immediate need.*

As the fluid rushed from the needle into my veins, I felt nothing at first and thought the heroin had failed me. I saw Mindy next to me, leaning against Jeff, while I nodded off as the warmth came over me. It felt like the first time – like being wrapped in a warm, secure blanket of happiness. The little devil man faded away, and I sensed all was right in my world. I would overcome everything tomorrow and be back where I belonged, with Lina and her family in their warm and loving home. I closed my eyes to savor the feeling.

Then, the warmth withdrew from me as if from a vacuum and was suddenly replaced by a painfully sharp coldness filling every inch of my body. It was worse than the cold seeping through my veins when I laid on the ground a few months before. My body quivered, and a numbness came over me, followed by darkness, then nothing.

Lina: *I received a call from the police saying Sterling was in the hospital. Nicki, Natalie, and Jay met me there and were all able to go to his room. The doctor explained that Sterling had overdosed, and he was barely hanging on to life. His brain scan showed no sign of life, and a machine was breathing for him.*

How I wish I could have done something more. I thought about our last visit when Nicki and I found him getting off the bus. Who would think we would come to treasure those few moments sitting on the park bench? I wish he had asked for help, but it was too late now. We all stood by his bedside talking, singing, and praying. Sterling's father was also in the room.

I was Sterling's health care proxy, but something was missing from the paperwork and they turned to Sterling's father to decide to pull the life support. I honestly didn't want to make that decision, so it may have been divine intervention when a legal issue meant I didn't have to.

It was just an hour after they pulled the plug when the priest had left the room. He continued to breathe, and Nicki, Natalie, and Jay left the room saying they couldn't watch him die. I came closer and whispered to him to let go. I instantly felt a change and knew he was released from his body. In that moment, I lost my precious son. My life would never be the same. The pain of losing Sterling would consume me for years to come.

The drug that had once taken away Sterling's pain had now taken his life. It deceived him in so many ways. He thought he could use it once more, but he was wrong. The drug stole everything from him.

Fortunately, this wasn't the same outcome for Mindy and Jeff. They both found recovery. Mindy went back home after

Sterling's overdose and admitted to her parents she needed help. They sent her to a long-term rehab facility followed by a sober home. Mindy is now married with twins and is living a sober life.

Jeff had a more difficult path, but he is living a sober life now. After multiple stays in a rehab facility, he finally found a place that gave him hope and direction. Now, he's a recovery coach and using his experience to help others find recovery. No one ever thought Jeff would find recovery. Now he shares a message: Recovery is possible, and you are worth it.

It's been eight years since Sterling's passing and so much has changed. We didn't know at the time, but addiction is a disease, and changes the function and chemistry of the brain. That's exactly what happened to him. I wish he would have admitted the truth to me. I would have helped him find the right treatment to fight this disease. I pray and hope Sterling's story keeps those of you who have never fallen victim to drugs from ever using, or helps those of you who have, find your healing, and helps you to believe in yourself. Jeff is right, "Recovery is possible, and you are worth it."

Clinician's comments

I had just completed graduate school and was recently licensed by the state as a mental health counselor when I was given my first client. He was an addict, and unbeknownst to me had been selling heroin to support his habit. He responded to the counseling and he got clean. For nearly 8 months, he had been doing well, and went back to high school as a senior. His relationship with his mother and sister improved, and he seemed happier. One weekend he was arrested for selling heroin and when he got out the next Monday, he was found dead of an overdose. His mother and sister were devastated, and I felt like a failure as a professional. He had a bipolar diagnosis and never missed taking his medication. It seemed as if he was always stable, but mental health, like recovery, is never a linear process and is prone to twists and turns.

The most difficult part of getting into treatment is finding the right place and the right time with an open bed. There is a finite amount of treatment slots in the community, with an infinite need for them. Sterling was on the verge of telling his friends he wanted to be clean but did not. In my experience, most addicts want to be clean, and will respect and support others who want to. Something must be said first.

Questions and discussion points

What could Lina have done differently?

Should she have been more aggressive in getting him help?

Do you recognize any of Sterling's personality traits or behavior in your friends or family members?

What affect did drinking have on Sterling's behavior? Did it make him weaker or stronger?

You can learn more about Sterling by reading *Living with the Little Devil Man*, by Lina Lisette.

Available on Amazon: https://amzn.to/3aCBAIJ

Lina's website: https://linalisetta.com/

THIS IS <u>MY</u> PROBLEM, NOT <u>YOURS</u>

Jeff

I started using heroin when I was 53 years old. Whenever I tell people, I get the same startled response, "What? At *that* age? Didn't you know better Jeff?" Not in my wildest dreams did I ever think I'd be a heroin addict. And what about all that stuff about *"Just Say No"* we've heard for decades? Isn't it what we told our kids to say when confronted with a choice? Shouldn't I have known better? Why was it so difficult for me to follow this straightforward instruction? Well, it's not always that simple.

What events could possibly bring a mature grandfather to use heroin?

First, I didn't fit into the stereotype – the box I thought drug addicts belonged in. I was a family guy, with kids and grandkids, and was safely removed from that type of activity. Drinking was my thing.

I had to have said "yes" to someone, right? I said yes to my doctors. When they prescribed OxyContin for my back pain, I followed their professional advice and did as instructed. In fact, I took *less* than prescribed at first, because I didn't need them. I was managing through it, and all was good. Until my next visit with the doctor.

Before I get into the details of what happened next, I should let you know that maybe all *wasn't* good after all. Starting back in high school and in my late teens, I did my share of drinking, graduated to cocaine, and eventually experimented with acid. I had no inhibitions because it seemed harmless at the time. And didn't everybody do it anyway?

I was content hanging out with friends, playing the guitar, working on cars, or going fishing once in a while. A lot changed when I met Donna. We got married in our early twenties and immediately started a family. Stella was born in 1979, then we were surprised with twins, Ann and Lily, in 1981. Our fourth daughter Sophia was born in 1982.

My job and family consumed me, but I still found time to play the guitar and work on my car, and all those activities were perfectly compatible with drinking. I enjoyed them more with a few beers. I was home, and it didn't bother anyone.

When socializing with family or friends, drinking wasn't ever a choice – it was expected. I could always stop if I wanted, but had no need to. There were lots of reasons, but I recognized none of them back then.

I got up every morning at 3:30 to drive a fork truck at the cement piping company, no matter the weather, and worked until mid to late afternoon. Despite the long days and physically demanding conditions, I was reliable as the sunrise and did it for twenty-two years.

Donna bore the greater burden of parenting. As hard as it was working outside in the cold dark mornings in January, dealing with four kids under five by yourself was much more difficult. When school came around, Donna got them all dressed, fed, and ready for the day – before she went to work herself. At the end of my workday, I made a point of spending time with my daughters, helping where I could, and seeing them off to bed. I never missed birthdays or special events.

My other interests faded, but I still found time to drink. One night of heavy drinking, I gave my guitar to my younger brother Jim, and I wasn't ever getting it back.

As a young and healthy, but sometimes reckless guy, I was fearless. One day in my early thirties, while pounding down a few too many at a birthday party, I was bouncing on a backyard trampoline doing back flips. *What could go wrong there?* Thinking I was half my age, I flipped off to the side and landed on the metal edge of the trampoline, and then fell flat on my back on the ground full force. While lying there my brother Jim leaned over and said, "What the hell's wrong with you Jeff? You still think you're 13?" I got up, shook it off and went back to drinking. A few hours later, stammered off to bed.

The next morning, I could hardly walk, but still made it to work Monday morning. The pain persisted, but I endured it without seeing a doctor. I lived with the soreness, but my back was never quite the same.

When we had family events, I often made myself scarce. They'd go without me or I'd find a little spot by myself to drink. Either way, I wasn't the best person to be around. Things went on like this for years. And although Donna and I would fight – mostly about my drinking issues and lack of family participation, I knew she'd never leave me. She said she didn't believe in divorce, so subconsciously I may have felt protected, and was acting without fear of consequence. Maybe I wanted to be alone after all; things would be easier, and I wouldn't have to catch shit just because I felt like drinking. Why she made such a big deal of it anyway pissed me off. It didn't affect her – Donna and the kids did all they wanted. If they would just let me be, we'd all be happy.

Life went on with schoolwork, sports events, birthdays, and sleepovers – filled in with tension, arguments, and lots of drinking. And of course, a widening distance between Donna and me. If she had just lightened up a little, things could have been so much easier. I was a responsible employee, provided for my family, and did what a father and husband are supposed to do – what more could anyone ask? I'm entitled to have a few beers. So what? My family and my drinking were under full control. Looking back, both were not.

It's what I want to do — it does not affect you. How many times do I need to get that through your head? It's not your problem, it's mine. Stay away, leave me alone, and we'll all be better off.
When I think of how many times I said this out loud to Donna, I shudder at the selfishness and disregard I had for those who loved and cared for me. After a fight I'd see the pain in her eyes as she ran into the other room crying, while I stubbornly shouted some underserved comment back. I'd feel bad for a minute, but it only gave me a reason to pour myself another beer.

I was in denial — not conscious denial, but with a dismissive *"This will just fade away and we'll all move on"* feeling. Another incident, another fight. Repeat the scene.

One Saturday, when I was about 45, a few friends and I were cutting down a large tree. I had roped off a section of the tree and held the rope tight to pull away as my friend began cutting. The rope snapped, and I was thrown backwards on to the ground. At the time I felt little pain, but the next morning was sheer agony and I knew I had a serious problem. It was like the trampoline pain but a hundred times worse.

This is when the whole thing started. The thing that turned our lives upside down forever.

This time I went to the doctor. I was older and not recovering the same way as ten years earlier. The problem, the doctor stated, was a herniated disk. He prescribed OxyContin and Tylenol. I took the oxy only as needed, along with the Tylenol, managed through the pain, and went back to work after a few days off.

At first this was working, and I took less pills than advised. When I went back to the doctor, he prescribed another bottle of forty-two more pills. I told him I had plenty left and didn't need them. He gave me a puzzled look and said that's not the way it's supposed to work.

He instructed me to take the pills as indicated to stay ahead of the pain, not to wait until I was reacting to it. I set another appointment for 4 weeks, went home, and did as the doctor requested. Why would I question his orders?

After about ten days of consistent use, the pills did nothing for me, and I was becoming intolerant. I found myself awake at night and sluggish during the day. Another visit, and another forty-two-pill script. I was also told to take acetaminophen for my gout.

I was getting frustrated, feeling crappy, and talked to a few friends at work about it. One of them suggested I crush the oxy pills and snort them. It would provide quicker relief from the sickness I was feeling. He also suggested combining the acetaminophen and the oxy to work more efficiently. I felt better, but later suffered headaches and nausea. Now I was going through the supply much quicker. I progressed from 40 to 80 to 200 milligrams a day, and my body became more intolerant of the higher dosage. The more I took, the more I needed to make the sickness go away. I was awake when I was supposed to be sleeping and sleeping when I was supposed to be awake. The days lost their structure, and I remember it just being dark a lot.

This all triggered a desperation – more like a severe panic – of getting more pills to stop it all. I needed the drugs in my body as soon as possible or I'd get unbearably ill. In fact, I'd never experienced such a terrible sickness in all my life. My body sweated and ached, and the combination of nausea and diarrhea was relentless. I couldn't tell if the sickness caused more anxiety and depression or the other way around, but it was overwhelming, and I would do anything to stop it. The term that describes this, which I learned later, was being "dope sick".

The more dope sick I got, the more I needed the drugs to feel normal. I knew nothing about addiction and would laugh at the mere notion of it. However, my brain was being programmed to require this drug to function.

I ran through my prescription and went back to the doctor for more. He questioned why I needed them so quickly, so I told him I was in a canoe and it tipped over and I lost all my pills. After a few probing questions and a skeptical look, he gave in and told me to be more careful. He saw right through me but gave me a chance I wouldn't get a second time. A guy I knew suggested copying the script for future use. He said all I'd have to do was change the date. I was reluctant, but made a copy anyway, just in case.

Enough time had gone by and I went back to the doctor to get another script. He didn't forget the canoe story, and of course he brought it up. He asked a few questions but halfway through my answers he abruptly said, "Never mind, I'm not writing this prescription for you."

"Why not?" I snapped back. "I need them!"

"You've been drinking, and anyone within ten feet of you can smell it. Go home Jeff."

He lectured me about the dangers of using alcohol and narcotics. Stunned and angry, I left the room before he finished. *I'll outsmart him*, I thought, as I remembered the copied script I had at home. I brought it to the pharmacy, and it worked, but just once. Next attempt I wasn't so lucky. Apparently, the doctor notified the pharmacy, or vice versa. I never knew, but it didn't matter.

I paid a heavy price for the prescription forgery. It's a federal offense, and I went to court, paid $5,000 for a lawyer, and was placed on probation for a year. I should have known better, but the sickness was so overpowering I gave in and didn't listen to my conscience.

With my legitimate supplier gone, I needed other resources. I couldn't get through the day without it, and thought of nothing else. Drugs first, drinking second, food a distant third. I was addicted and didn't know it. With some digging, I found some people to buy from on the streets. The more I used, the more I needed, and my daily dose went from 200 to 400 mg a day, and that didn't come cheap. For a while this was working, and I didn't get sick from it. I only got sick if I *didn't* have it. I wasn't using to get high – only to stay normal. It not only took the aches and pains away, but the stress and anxiety too. The pills became ineffective, so I kept increasing to a point where it was costing a couple thousand dollars a month to maintain.

Life was changing around me, but I didn't seem to notice. Or care. My excellent work ethic went from bad to worse, and I eventually lost my job. I blew more money on drugs, and my family relations were suffering. I became lethargic, irresponsible, and no longer recognized who I was.

Donna and I were fighting, and after many threats to kick me out of the house, she finally did. I went to a rehab, then after a few weeks would begin using again. I was simply too preoccupied with drugs and not strong enough to overcome the addiction. Drugs were my full priority. I even sold my tools just to get more drugs.

Donna: *Our daughters, who had all moved out on their own, said I was enabling their father, and they all told me repeatedly that I should kick him out and divorce him. It was the only way he'd change, they said. I told them I wanted to keep trying, and I wasn't giving up. But Jeff was dismantling our household, in more ways than one. I'd find things missing, only to realize later he was selling anything he could get his hands on just to get money to buy drugs. I couldn't understand his behavior, and he no longer resembled the man I married.*

I was taking everything away from our family. So many promises made, and even more broken. In and out of detox, back in rehab, back to my old ways… this went on for years. After enduring this nonsense, who would ever want to deal with me? Pushing the limits of Donna's patience, I was slowly breaking her. I always loved Donna, but the drugs took complete control and I loved them more. I needed them, craved them, and nothing else was remotely as important. Not even close.

I went to buy some oxy from my usual guy and told him how sick I was. He said he didn't have any, and I freaked out on him. He told me to calm down, and said he had something else to would make me feel better. He pulled out a few small bags of heroin and said it would take care of everything. I told him I knew nothing about heroin, but he insisted it would work, and gave me three small bags. I snorted through a small straw and waited a few seconds. An instant rush went through my blood and I got a little dizzy. My head was spinning, and I wanted to throw up. The only thing I thought was, *Why would anyone ever want to do this?* After being dope sick so much, this wasn't the cure I expected. The guy told me I'd get over it quickly and suggested I try again. I was easily persuaded, and desperate to make the dope sickness go away.

He was right, and from that point on heroin was my friend. After the instant rush of euphoria, it warmed every inch of my body like being hugged by a warm blanket. Tension and pain disappeared in a whoosh. I snorted at first, but once I tried the needle I didn't go back. I loved the needle, and the instant gratification it provided.

I soon graduated to doing speedball, a mix of cocaine and heroin, to enhance the effect. The stimulating effects of cocaine would cancel out the depressant of the heroin – the perfect cocktail. My habit jumped from two thousand dollars a month to over three thousand.

The dealers on the street were always saying they had a better quality product than the previous stuff I bought. There were "brands" with their own special stamp on the bag with their color, usually blue or red. Some were called batman or superman, and each had varying amounts of fentanyl. If a particular brand had a reputation for causing deadly overdoses, you would think it would be a warning to stay away. Ironically, the opposite was true. The extra strength takes you that much closer to the ultimate high, and risks aren't considered. The high quality "good stuff" brought you to the edge of death, or sometimes beyond it. The demand was high, business was competitive, and the dealers fought for their share of customers by luring them with a "premium product." The risk of death is often shrugged off for a chance at the best high possible.

I was lying a lot to Donna, and disappeared for hours, sometimes days. She'd get on my case and I'd say it was my problem, and none of her concern. "I'm doing this to me – NOT you!" I'd shout out. To say I was selfish is an understatement. Under my drug induced state, I believed this was true. This delusion granted me a license to continue drinking and using drugs. It's amazing what you can convince yourself of, or how brilliantly creative you suddenly become. Or so you think. I thought I could fool people – everyone from my family, to doctors, to people I worked with, even myself. But at every turn I was proven not so clever. I went back to the streets to get my heroin and worked up to four bags a day, spending any spare money I had.

Donna: *Jeff was rummaging through the house looking for things to sell and I tried to stop him. I called the police, and when they arrived, they said since we were married, he had as much right to our possessions as I did, and the only way to stop him was to get divorced. Our daughters also insisted I initiate a divorce, which was painful to hear from them. It went against everything I stood for, but I felt increasing pressure to end our marriage, and I was left with no option. I was forced to betray my own belief that a marriage is forever and was angry it came to that. With everything I had I tried to save our marriage, but the pain Jeff put us through was unimaginable, and I couldn't endure any more. Legally it was the only way to protect what we had left,*

*and I still thought maybe then Jeff may get the help he needed.
I never imagined life without Jeff, and here I was forced to do
the unthinkable.*

Donna reached a breaking point, and she kicked me out
again. While stuffing my clothes in a large green trash bag, she
said the words I never thought I'd hear, "I'm divorcing you.
You need to go now!"

I was devastated, and went straight to my parent's house.
They took me in, but of course they weren't thrilled about it.
It was either their house, or a homeless shelter. Or a bed at the
detox center. Which is where they convinced me to go. So off
to the Providence Behavioral Health Center in Holyoke I went.
In the meantime, Donna initiated the divorce, and I didn't have
the financial or mental capacity to fight it.

My parents weren't quite aware of the heroin habit, only the
drinking. I lied to them too. I tried to get clean – my intentions
were good – but I could not overcome the addiction. At the
center I told them whatever I had to say to get into the
methadone clinic. After a few weeks I was getting sick, so the
doctor gave me a fentanyl patch and I immediately broke out
in hives. They gave me Vivitrol to block the effect of the
heroin, but the sickness wouldn't go away. A few weeks later,
I went back to my parent's house.

Over the next year and a half, I bounced between the detox
center, rehabs, and my parents' house. I went to one Christian
rehab for seven months and thought I was making progress.
But again, I was too weak to fight against the powers of the
drug.

I went to another local sober house for three months and
shared a small room with two sets of bunk beds and three
bunkmates. A common bathroom down the hall
accommodated all sixteen residents. Downstairs was a kitchen
where I could prepare meals I bought with food stamps. The
living room / meeting room had a TV everyone would fight

over. They required us to attend at least three meetings a week. This was a miserable and depressing time. How could I have gone from being a providing husband and father, to bunking with smelly strangers, using food stamps, and fighting over the most trivial things? *Who moved my stuff? That's my chair! Who drank my juice?* That's what dominated our days. Nobody there gave a shit about me unless I had drugs for them. I was angry, and all my new roommates were too.

I got out and tried to stay sober, but it didn't last. The withdrawal was wreaking havoc in my body. The only thing I knew, or cared about, is that I felt sick without the drugs. I didn't want to be sick, so it seemed natural, and easier, to feed the brain and body.

This is how it went, an endless loop, like the Groundhog Day movie. Except, rather than wake up in the same bed over and over, I found myself in a detox bed, a rehab unit, a group home, or a shelter. The nightmare only deepened.

The divorce was final in April of 2018, two months shy of our 40th anniversary. I missed my family terribly and never felt so alone, so separated from everyone. It couldn't get any worse than this, and I wanted to escape, but to where? I thought it would be easier for everyone if I wasn't around at all.

I drove around Holyoke looking for a quiet place to shoot up. One place after another wouldn't work, so I impatiently pulled the car over on Race Street by the canal. It was around mid-day, and clusters of people were going about their business, paying no attention to me. *This will have to work*, I thought, *I can't wait any longer.*

I had no idea, no inkling, that this would be my final injection. With the needle prepared, I rolled up my sleeve, put the band on my bicep, and inserted the needle. I pushed the syringe, and watched the mixture disappear into my vein. A quick tug and the needle dropped to the floor as my eyes rolled back into my head. I was out, with no sense of light or darkness. Entirely departed from all existence.

The sound of heavy breathing was the first thing I remember, like an amplified ventilator machine, pulling air in and pushing back out. With my eyes still closed, the only sensation I had was my chest forcefully expanding and contracting, getting louder with each labored breath. My eyes opened slowly until the blurry images came into focus. I sat motionless, not knowing if I was dead or alive. I had no sense of time, and didn't know where I was or how I got there.

My eyes scanned the area, it appeared to be late afternoon, and I recognized the factories and the canal. It was all coming back now. *I'm still in this damn car.* The syringe on the floor told me all I needed to know. The people I had seen earlier were gone, the street void of any activity. Gone too were the cars parked in front and behind me. *How long have I been here? Four, maybe five hours?* My heart raced with so many questions running through my mind. *Who saw me here? What if someone had called the police?* For sure, some passerby would have noticed a guy slouched in his car for hours and thought he was dead and called the police. Yet I was left to die alone. Perhaps I did die, and somehow God spared me and gave me a second chance.

The more I thought about it, the more scared I became. I couldn't move a muscle in my body, as if all my circulation had vacated my extremities and flooded my chest to keep my heart and lungs operating. *Just breathe*, I commanded myself. *Just breath and listen.* I closed my eyes again, focused on my breathing, and thanked God I was alive. A voice came from somewhere deep inside me, a voice *felt* more than heard, saying it wasn't about me anymore. It was about Donna, Stella, Ann, Lily, and Sophia. How would they feel if I was found dead by some old factory along a canal from a heroin overdose?

It's a hell of a thing to leave your kids with a lifelong trauma they'd have to explain to their children. My grandkids should not have a dead heroin addict grandfather. The reality of dying hit me in the face so hard I couldn't catch my breath.

Overwhelmed with fear, shame, and sadness, I welled up with tears and began shaking uncontrollably. I resolved then not to have my wife and daughters think of me in this way – their last memory of Dad as a heroin addict.

How many years had I lost? How much have I hurt my family? There was no more time to waste. No more pain to cause. I needed to salvage my family and live again.

I called my daughter Lily and she may have sensed it was the right time to talk. She told me about the Celebrate Recovery program at her church. Yes, I said, without asking too many questions. I was defeated, and more than ready for the journey back to permanent sobriety. I had yet to learn *how*.

That fateful day in the car by the canal could have been my last. It is, in fact, where my old life ended. Recovery is a forever journey, and I am fully aware of the dangers of relapse, and know there are no guarantees in life.

I think of opiate drugs as the work of the devil. I am certain of it. It's like being possessed by a demon with the most evil deception imaginable. To me, the image that captures it best is the last scene of Raiders of the Lost Ark, when the bad guys open the ark. The image of a beautiful angel appears, and they're all struck with awe and amazement, and shout out, "It's so beautiful!" When they all fall under its spell, the face turns demonic and they all die horribly. Unfortunately, too many addicts have reached their fatal point of no return.

It's no different with opiates. They deceive you into thinking it's paradise, but it's really hell. They will suck every ounce of life out of you, maybe slowly or quickly, but it gets the job done. It always goes down the same path of sickness, isolation, anxiety, depression, or death - nothing but dark horrible outcomes that ruin lives. There is no life, no family, nor any situation that has ever been improved by the use of heroin or other opioid drugs.

I lived with my parents, went to meetings, and stayed sober. I was taking Vivitrol for a while, but the side effects made my body ache. It was still better than the sickness from withdrawal. I had to earn back the trust from my daughters, and even though Donna and I were divorced, I wanted to prove to all of them that I could do it. Donna wasn't taking me back, but she tried to be supportive for the sake of our daughters and grandchildren.

I tried to talk with Donna about the steps I was taking toward recovery but she wasn't buying it. After the countless times I broke promises, and failed her and our daughters, it was too painful, and she didn't want to suffer through anymore relapses and heartache. She reminded me that we divorced for a reason, and I was no longer the person she married. She said she still didn't trust my commitment to remain sober.

Donna: *I never wanted the divorce, but I never wanted our lives turned upside down either. It broke my heart, but I told Jeff we had to stay apart. Even through all the difficult times, I knew it was the drugs talking not him. It was someone else, like something evil had taken over. I believed Jeff when he said he wanted to stay sober and get back to who he was, but I also knew his actions would have to speak louder than his words.*

I understood Donna's position, and had to respect it. But I was alive, and grateful to God every day for giving me another chance. Every day is a gift, and every day sober brings me closer to earning back trust of my family. From that moment of Lily bringing up Celebrate Recovery, I haven't looked back. It has been my lifeline, and I hope to help others get through the hell of addiction and emerge with a productive and happy life the same way the loving and caring people there helped me. If I can do it after fifteen years of addiction, I know there is hope for anyone. But there is one thing I know, it cannot be done without the support and love of family, friends, and support groups.

Donna slowly allowed me to see her and our daughters more often, and even had me over for dinner once in a while. When we were together, we talked and laughed like we haven't in years, maybe decades. Life looked different through sober eyes, and I couldn't remember having so much clarity in my brain and my heart. I began to spend more time at home, attended church, and continued with the program at Celebrate Recovery.

I brought up an idea that Donna flatly rejected. I wanted to get married again. She said the thought of it terrified her, and said no. I wanted my family back, but wanted them to want *me* back as much as I did. I knew it wasn't going to be easy, but I resolved to work at it with every ounce of strength I had and wasn't giving up.

Donna: *During the first year or so of Jeff's recovery I was encouraged, but remained skeptical. After so many years — decades, not years — of drinking and drugs, I was hardened, and not easily convinced. So many times he would promise it would never happen again. And it always happened again. I made it clear to him that earning back my trust wasn't like a switch I could turn on just because he promised something. I wasn't sure when, or if, that would ever happen. One year of being clean wasn't going to erase fifteen years of torture. I would always have to be prepared for the day he would fall back, and told him I could never go through it again.*

Earlier I mentioned that you can't overcome addiction without the love and support of family, friends, and support groups. That's true, but in my case, I could not do it without faith in the power of God. I was without it for so much of my life. I was spiritually vacant and didn't know it. When I accepted God's help, everything changed. When I was going through years of addiction, the last thing I thought about was God. Me – that's who I thought about. I blamed everyone else: the doctor, my family... everyone but me. No one else brought this on but me.

My personal feeling is you don't have to hit bottom before seeking help. People don't need to lose everything before being motivated to change. It's just more wasted years, more damaged relationships, and a deeper financial hole. Oh, how I wished I could have known this and changed at the beginning. But I am sober now, and that matters more than anything. I choose for it to be more powerful than the addiction, more powerful than any regret, guilt, or temptation. I am sustained and supported by the power of love and faith in God. Nothing is stronger.

Donna: *Something had changed with Jeff. In the past, whenever a stressful situation arose, I sensed the usual "trigger" and his desire to use drugs or drink as an escape. Now it was different, and he was engaged, focused, and confident. It was truly a remarkable transformation. The difference was that God was now present in our lives. The man I married was returning.*

Jeff asked me again to marry him again, and I finally said yes. We were re-married on June 30th, 2020, our 42nd anniversary. Our daughters and grandchildren were there, and I thank God every day that we have our family back, and for the miracle of Jeff's recovery.

Learning how to live clean is more than just stopping drug use. It's re-learning to do all the things in life sober that you got used to doing under the influence of alcohol or drugs. Basic things like family relations, friends, financial responsibilities, and being emotionally connected. It may sound easy, but sometimes you have no idea how much damage is done until you try to repair what had been broken for years, or even decades.

I almost lost everything, but I am standing where I never thought I would. And I pray my story will help prevent someone else from going down the same destructive path.

Clinician's comments

Jeff's story is a familiar one. So many clients reveal they had a problem with alcohol or some other underlying condition long before they turned to drug use. We often fail to look at the cultural pressures in our lives, and respond with alcohol consumption as "normal", "routine", or "expected." It isn't perceived as a problem because "everyone does it".

With the rise of the opioid epidemic, we have realized that doctors prescribed addictive pain medications in larger doses and for longer periods than were appropriate without sounding the warnings about addictive properties associated with these "treatments".

In Jeff's case, we can clearly see the cycle of drug dependence develop and completely overwhelm his sense of family, work, and personal freedom. Drugs "rewire" the brain, and that is why we call it a brain disease. The reward center of the brain called the limbic system takes over the decision-making process and allows our thoughts, feelings, and behaviors to be driven by the drug and the cycle of addiction it brings. We will do or say things we never thought possible to keep the addiction going. Jeff was fortunate he survived an overdose. The fact that it scared the life out him wasn't a bad thing. He did not leave his family devastated with his death, but instead, it set him on a path to recovery with his family's support.

Questions and discussion points

If you were Jeff's wife, what would you do differently?

Would you remain supportive under these circumstances?

When Jeff admitted he loved the drugs more than his family, how do you think his wife and daughters felt?

What thoughts went through Jeff as he woke up in the car?

Should Jeff's parents have taken him in?

Would a family meeting have helped by making sure everyone was consistent in their reaction to Jeff's behavior?

A CLINICIAN'S PERSPECTIVE

by *Chris Bernier, M.Ed. LMHC LSW CADCII*

Addiction is brain disease. The chemicals that make someone "feel good" or "feel better" change the microscopic nerve endings. It physically alters the way people think, feel, and behave. As demonstrated in the preceding stories, the addicts become different people entirely, almost unrecognizable to their own family members.

Once someone has been using drugs or alcohol, only they can tell if they are an addict or alcoholic because it is different for everyone. Recovery is a similar process, and it is more than just being sober. To learn to live and do daily tasks without having to rely on drug or alcohol to get through it is a large part of treatment and as a clinician in the field, it helps to figure out where someone is at and go from there.

As a clinician, I need to determine how drug use is potentially influencing someone's life negatively and what services or treatment would be available to this person if they wanted the help. I start with an assessment. That assessment could come in a few forms but will ask some basic questions such as:

Is the drug use negatively affecting their family, work, school, or social life?

Do they have cravings or a strong desire to use?

Have they developed a tolerance to the drug?

Are they spending a great deal of time trying to get the drug or recover from its effects?

Do they use in situations where they could get physically hurt?

Are they taking more of the drug than they intended, or for longer periods than intended?

Are important relationships in their life suffering because of the drug use?

Have they been unsuccessful at trying to stop of their own?

Have they gone into withdrawals?

If the answer is yes to just two of these questions, then there is enough to have concern that someone has a substance abuse disorder and that they need help.

If you think you need help for yourself or a loved one, it's ok to talk to a trained professional first. 1-800-662-HELP (4357) is the national hotline for people in need. There are crisis teams usually assigned to every major hospital in many US cities, and there are local clinics that can be accessed by simply dialing 211 on any phone in the state that you need help in.

You might save yourself some time by looking to see who has a treatment bed available by visiting https://www.mabhaccess.com/Search.aspx. This database is updated every 6 hours by the treatment providers in detoxes, residential programs, Transition support treatment centers, etc. around the state of Massachusetts. Many other states have similar databases or lists of programs available and they can be found by visiting https://www.samhsa.gov/programs or by simply calling the 800 number above.

If you need support for yourself because a family member is struggling with an addiction there are groups that can help. Al-anon has a listing of family support groups that may be helpful. Their national number is 1-888-4AL-ANON

About Chris Bernier M.Ed. LMHC LSW CADCII

Chris is licensed by the state of Massachusetts as a mental health counselor, social worker and drug and alcohol counselor. He has over 20 years working the field of addiction and mental health with children, adolescents and adults in a variety of levels of care. He has worked at a local behavioral health hospital in the Holyoke area, and had served as a director at a community corrections outpatient treatment center for adults in the criminal justice system and has worked with DUI offenders in an outpatient treatment program in both Connecticut and Massachusetts. Chris has also worked as a consultant for several substance and mental health organizations in the Springfield area providing clinical guidance and supervision to clinical staff. Chris currently works for a local behavioral health organization and is assigned as the court clinician working with four specialty treatment courts in western Massachusetts. He graduated with his bachelor's in behavioral psychology from Western New England College and completed his master's in psychology focusing on mental health from Springfield College.

RESOURCES

Substance Abuse and Mental Health Services Administration
www.samhsa.gov

Alcoholics Anonymous
www.aa.org

Narcotics Anonymous
www.na.org

12-step family support
www.al-anon.org or www.nar-anon.org

SMART Recovery
www.smartrecovery.org

Celebrate Recovery
www.celebraterecovery.com
Celebrate Recovery is a national Christian-based 12-Step recovery program that meets weekly. If you are experiencing anger, addiction, bitterness, codependency, anxiety, depression, or shame, you will find hope and healing here. Go to the Celebrate Recovery website to find a meeting in your area.

Local Celebrate Recovery programs in western Massachusetts are listed on the following page.

Springfield Rescue Mission
www.springfieldrescuemission.org

Compass Recovery Center
975a Springfield St. Feeding Hills, MA 01030
844.844.2978
www.compassrecoverytreatment.com

Celebrate Recovery programs in Hampden County, MA:

LifePoint Church
603 New Ludlow Rd., Chicopee, MA
413-563-2775
Marilyn & George Ekimovich, Ministry Directors

Hope for Holyoke
100 Suffolk Street, Holyoke, MA 01020
413-561-1020, Debbie Gonzalez

Bethany Assembly of God
580 Main Street, Agawam, MA 01001
413-789-2930
Teresa Sanchez, Woman's Director
Jim Corker, Men's Director

Evangelical Covenant Church
915 Plumtree Rd. Springfield, MA 01119
413-782-5212, www.eccspringfield.org

Our Father's House Ministry Center
938 Chicopee St. Chicopee, MA 01013
(413) 768-0916, Peggy Jackman

ABOUT THE AUTHOR

Michael K. Tourville lives in Agawam, Massachusetts with his wife Chiara. Tourville is the Sales and Marketing Director for Evans Cooling Systems, Inc., based out of Connecticut.

His first book, *A Promise to Astrid*, was an award-winning true story, turned into a movie in 2018, and starring Dean Cain and JoAnn F. Peterson. *Voices from the Fallen* is his second book.

Mike has four grandchildren, Lily, Bryn, Nick, and Mikey from his son Bill and daughter-in-law Angela. Mike's younger son Nick and his fiancé Beth currently live in Virginia.

Please read on for an excerpt of
Mike Tourville's first book,

A Promise to Astrid

No one else would be calling this late. I should have left the office hours before, which meant it could only be one person. The ringing seemed amplified, as if the phone itself was shouting at me to pick up. I naturally assumed my wife Cindy was a little annoyed at my thoughtlessness, and our two young boys, Billy and Nick, were anxious for me to arrive home. It was a warm summer night in early July 1986, and here I was wasting valuable family time at work. Anticipating Cindy's displeasure, I closed my eyes, took a deep breath, and picked up the phone.

I didn't even say hello. Never had the chance. The instant the receiver was lifted, I heard Cindy's frantic voice telling me she had just been in a car accident.

Still shaken, she explained in an overly excited, rapid-fire delivery:

"Mike, the guy hit my car hard and I didn't see him and he went through a red light because mine was green and the car is smashed and the guy in the van didn't tell the truth."

Each word ran into the next in one continual exhaling stream of information until she ran out of breath.

"All right, calm down," I said. "Where are you?"

I managed to get a word in, but it only served to allow Cindy a much-needed oxygen recharge. She normally talked fast, but she was setting new speed records here.

"I'm home, the cops gave me a ride the car was towed and he lied to the cop because both lights can't be green so they gave me a ticket instead of him and then. . . "

My mind was working as quickly as possible to process this information in split seconds. It was like trying to put a jigsaw puzzle together while the pieces are being tossed at you. I forcefully wedged in a few questions to break her relentless crescendo.

"Cindy, slow down. Are you alright? Are the boys with you?"

"I'm fine," she said in a more composed manner. "Billy and Nick were at the neighbor's house, they weren't in the car."

"Ok, I'm coming home right now."

By the time I got home, Cindy was able to calmly explain what had happened. A van had raced through a red light and crashed into Cindy's 1980 Dodge Omni hatchback. The damage was extensive, but fortunately, she wasn't hurt. The other driver insisted his light was green, hoping the police would cite her and not him, and his plan worked.

I asked Cindy why she didn't tell her version to the police at the scene. She said she was nervous, and that the guy in the van was huge with an awful menacing look on his face. "I was scared and couldn't think straight," she said. "Everything happened so fast."

Those details didn't seem so critical at the time though, because the mere fact that Cindy came out of this accident without injury was a miracle. The driver couldn't have aimed any better; if a target was painted on the center of Cindy's door, he'd have hit a bulls-eye. The car was a complete wreck, but Cindy didn't have a scratch on her.

A few days later, I went to the police station to dispute her citation. Going through a red light and causing an accident was a serious violation and we didn't want that on her record. Cindy is honest to a fault, and I knew she told me the truth. She did not deserve a ticket for driving through a green light and finding herself in the path of a reckless driver.

The officer patiently listened to my entire argument, along with diagrams of the scene, and eventual pleas for reversal of the ticket. Before he could answer, I asked what steps we need to take in order to appeal the ticket. Politely and patiently allowing me to finish, he flatly said, "Well, what you say makes perfect sense, but your wife obviously doesn't feel so strongly about fighting the ticket."

I was puzzled. "What do you mean?"

"Looks like she sent a check and paid the ticket. I think this case is closed."

When I got home I asked Cindy why she sent a check right away. "You know," she said, "I don't like having things not paid, and on the back of the ticket it said we had to pay within twenty days. I didn't want it to be late and get in trouble."

"Yes, that is one option," I acknowledged. "But Cindy, there is another choice. One that says if you want to dispute the ticket, check this box."

"Uh oh," she said, "Does that mean . . .?"

"Yes, that's what it means. Paying a ticket is an admission of fault."

"Oh, no," she said, "I'm sorry." She shook her head, dropping her forehead into her hands saying, "Why did I do that?"

I always admired Cindy's ability to keep our bills up to date. But not this time.

Billy was in kindergarten, while Nick, three years younger, was at home. If Cindy were to get a full-time job, we'd have to pay for Nick's daycare, but we couldn't afford it as there weren't any jobs that paid well enough to make it feasible.

While adding up our bills one evening, Cindy had a bright idea. "What if," she said, with a rare pause to collect her thoughts, "What if I run a daycare here in the house?"

"Where?" I asked, "We don't have any room."

"We can clean out the basement, get a carpet, make a playroom, a nap room, and get some toys and. . ."

She went into great detail as if she'd planned it out for months. Maybe she had and was finally expressing her suppressed idea. The first thing I thought of was the disruption in the house; more kids running around, more toys to trip over, more commotion, and less privacy. I wasn't completely against the idea, but needed time to process the pros and cons.

In a short time, we were running a daycare and it turned out to be a tremendous help. Cindy was home when Billy came home from school, and we never had to think about daycare for Nick.

The extra money helped, but any unforeseen incident such as a broken appliance, car repair or any loss of income, would put us in quite a predicament. We certainly were not prepared to deal with the aftermath of an untimely car accident.

Compounding the problem, our inexperience in certain matters led us to make a few dumb decisions and bad judgments that cost us money we didn't have. To put it another way, we were young and stupid. Some things needed to change, and they were about to. In ways we never imagined.

Made in the USA
Monee, IL
14 February 2021